Beginning Writer's
Thesaurus

ScottForesman

A Division of HarperCollins*Publishers*

Editorial Offices: Glenview, Illinois
Regional Offices: Sunnyvale, California
Tucker, Georgia • Glenview, Illinois
Oakland, New Jersey • Dallas, Texas

ISBN 0-673-12378-2

89-RRC-99989796

Table of Contents

To the Teacher

Children are naturally curious about their world—including their world of words. ScottForesman's *Beginning Writer's Thesaurus* offers an excellent way to satisfy and nurture this curiosity. It helps students build their vocabularies while they learn how to recognize distinctions among words whose meanings are closely related.

ScottForesman's *Beginning Writer's Thesaurus* is a resource that can help students to express themselves with clarity and precision in their own writing. As such, it enables them to share with others what they know, what they see, what they feel, and what they imagine.

The entry words were carefully chosen for their frequency of use in spoken and written English. The synonyms included in the entries expand the beginning writer's stock of words. For example, synonyms for *bright,* such as *shiny, brilliant, radiant, sunny, glowing,* and *dazzling,* capture particular meanings and can add variety to a piece of writing. As students draw from a richer repertoire of words, they use language more confidently and proficiently.

This thesaurus presents information in ways that are designed to appeal to the beginning writer. Each entry word is defined in easy-to-understand language and shown in an example sentence or two. Synonyms for the entry words are also accompanied by short definitions and example sentences. Antonyms are included when appropriate, as well as cross-references for words with related meanings. Hundreds of pictures not only help students learn, but make learning more fun too.

In addition, the *Beginning Writer's Thesaurus* introduces various aspects of English-language usage and history. It also offers helpful hints for students to follow when writing.

▼••• **WRITER'S CHOICE** provides brief excerpts from works by popular and respected writers. The examples show effective word choice and point out why a particular synonym is the right one for the situation.

▼••• **WORDS AT PLAY** presents enjoyable verses using synonyms.

▼••• **WORD STORY** gives concise historical background about certain words.

▼••• **WRITING TIP** offers helpful "how-to's," such as how to avoid overused words and how to choose a synonym with the appropriate suggested meaning for a particular context.

▼••• **WORD WORKSHOP** presents mini-lessons that provide models for the revision process, improving writing samples by using precise synonyms.

▼••• **WORD POOL** provides a vocabulary-building collection of words that, although not synonyms, are related in some way, such as ways of running *(lope, jog, dash, sprint)* or kinds of bread *(muffin, bagel, tortilla)*.

▼••• **WORDS FROM WORDS**, another vocabulary-building feature, takes a base word, such as *play,* and combines it with affixes and other base words: *playmate, playhouse, plaything, playback, replay,* and so on.

▼••• **P.S.** is a feature that highlights idioms and other interesting aspects of our language.

The Introduction shows how to use this thesaurus, how each entry is organized, and what each feature contains.

An essay on increasing creativity comes after the main body of the thesaurus. It is followed by a Writer's Guide that offers tips on planning, writing, revising, and proofreading.

Finally, the thesaurus has three indexes: one of all entry words and synonyms (which includes the pronunciation for each listing), one of idioms and phrasal verbs, and one of special features.

Young writers have a lot to say, and ScottForesman's *Beginning Writer's Thesaurus* has been created to help them discover how to say it. We hope that you and your students find it useful.

Introduction

A Gift of Words

September 9

Dear Aunt Gloria,

Thank you for the nice surprise. I'm glad your dog had puppies. I named the one you gave me Tuffy.

Tuffy and I take nice walks together. He is nice to the little boy who lives next door. Even when the cat teases him, Tuffy is nice.

It was nice of you to give me such a nice puppy.

Love,

Mario

• Can you find a word that Mario uses too many times?

September 17

Dear Mario,

    Tuffy is a wonderful name for the dog. I'm delighted that you are enjoying him. He seemed like a friendly, good-natured puppy to me.

    I'm sending you a book of synonyms called a thesaurus. A synonym is a word that means almost the same as another word.

    A thesaurus is a valuable tool for writers. It can help you avoid using the same word over and over again. It can point you to the exact word you need. It can even introduce you to new words.

    I hope you will enjoy using your new thesaurus.

Love,

Aunt Gloria
Aunt Gloria

• Why do you think Aunt Gloria sent Mario the thesaurus? Look at Mario's letter. Also carefully reread Aunt Gloria's letter for a clue to her purpose.

• Why might a thesaurus be called "a gift of words"?

Understanding a Thesaurus Entry

Mario's thesaurus lists word studies in alphabetical order, but it is different from a dictionary in some important ways.

Although the thesaurus gives a meaning and synonyms for that meaning, it doesn't provide all the different meanings of a word that a dictionary does. Also, the thesaurus doesn't have as many entry words as most dictionaries, yet it provides some other kinds of information.

Use the entry for *afraid* on the next page to learn about the information included in the different parts of a thesaurus entry.

- The entry word is shown in large type at the left, near the top of the page. What word appears in small type immediately after the entry word? What information does this word provide?

- Look at the paragraph next to the entry for *afraid*. The first sentence gives the meaning of *afraid*. What is it?

- An example or examples printed in italic type follow the meaning to show how the word can be used in a sentence. How many example sentences are given for *afraid?*

- What synonyms are listed for *afraid?*

- Cross-references show other words listed in the thesaurus that have related but somewhat different meanings. What entry would you use to find words for the feeling of being afraid?

- Antonyms are words that have opposite meanings. What is an antonym for *afraid?*

- What additional information do you find under "Word Story"?

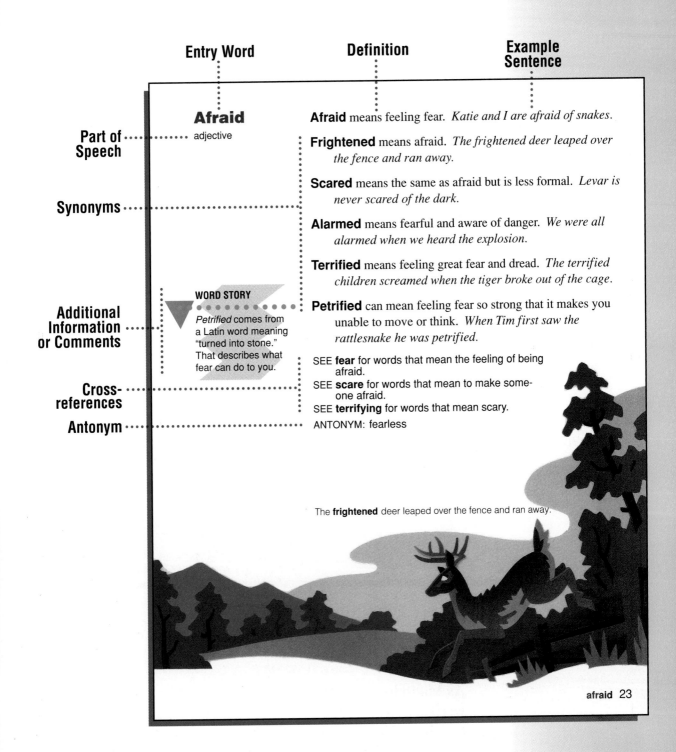

Entry Word

Definition

Example Sentence

Afraid
adjective

Part of Speech

Synonyms

Additional Information or Comments

Cross-references

Antonym

Afraid means feeling fear. *Katie and I are afraid of snakes.*

Frightened means afraid. *The frightened deer leaped over the fence and ran away.*

Scared means the same as afraid but is less formal. *Levar is never scared of the dark.*

Alarmed means fearful and aware of danger. *We were all alarmed when we heard the explosion.*

Terrified means feeling great fear and dread. *The terrified children screamed when the tiger broke out of the cage.*

Petrified can mean feeling fear so strong that it makes you unable to move or think. *When Tim first saw the rattlesnake he was petrified.*

WORD STORY

Petrified comes from a Latin word meaning "turned into stone." That describes what fear can do to you.

SEE **fear** for words that mean the feeling of being afraid.

SEE **scare** for words that mean to make someone afraid.

SEE **terrifying** for words that mean scary.

ANTONYM: fearless

The **frightened** deer leaped over the fence and ran away.

afraid 23

9

September 28

Dear Aunt Gloria,

    Thank you for the gift. I write lots of stories in school. The thesaurus will help me do a good job.

    I just read about a contest. The writers of the three best ads for a new kind of cereal will get prizes. If I work hard and use my thesaurus, I may get first prize, a trip to New York.

    You wouldn't believe how big Tuffy is! He already knows how to get a ball when I throw it. Learning a new trick gets Tuffy a treat.

    Love,

    Mario

Above is a letter Mario wrote to thank Aunt Gloria for the thesaurus.

As Mario looked over his letter, he noticed he had used the word *get* or *gets* four times. Mario didn't usually revise letters, but he wanted to try out his new thesaurus. He opened it to the letter *G* and found the word *get*, where seven synonyms were listed: *obtain, acquire, receive, fetch, win, earn,* and *gain.*

September 28

Dear Aunt Gloria,

 Thank you for the gift. I write lots of stories in school. The thesaurus will help me do a good job.

 I just read about a contest. The writers of the three best ads for a new kind of cereal will ~~get~~ receive *prizes. If I work hard and use my thesaurus, I may ~~get~~* win *first prize, a trip to New York.*

 You wouldn't believe how big Tuffy is! He already knows how to ~~get~~ fetch *a ball when I throw it. Learning a new trick ~~gets~~* earns *Tuffy a treat.*

 Love,

 Mario

This is the way Mario improved his letter. Notice the four synonyms he used in place of *get*.

You can find definitions and example sentences for the entry word *get* and its synonyms on page 86 of this thesaurus.

Using Cross-References

▼ •

Mario read his revised letter again. This time he noticed the word *good* in the first paragraph. He thought that the word *good* sounded boring.

Under the entry for *good*, Mario found the synonyms *fine* and *excellent*. These words made sense with the word *job*, but he decided first to check the cross-reference to *great*. Under the entry word *great*, Mario found just the right synonym to describe the kind of job he planned to do—*terrific*.

September 28

Dear Aunt Gloria,

    Thank you for the gift. I write lots of stories in school. The thesaurus will help me do a ~~good~~ *terrific* job.

    I just read about a contest. The writers of the three best ads for a new kind of cereal will ~~get~~ *receive* prizes. If I work hard and use my thesaurus, I may ~~get~~ *win* first prize, a trip to New York.

    You wouldn't believe how big Tuffy is! He already knows how to ~~get~~ *fetch* a ball when I throw it. Learning a new trick ~~gets~~ *earns* Tuffy a treat.

    Love,

    Mario

Features in Your Thesaurus

Every thesaurus lists synonyms. This thesaurus also has some special features to help you add sparkle to your writing, as well as learn some new words. One of these features is shown below. Other features are illustrated on the pages that follow. The Features Index on page 234 will help you find where these features appear in your thesaurus.

WRITER'S CHOICE

Writers of books you enjoy reading are good at using just the right words. Some words are better choices than others because they help set a mood or describe a character. The Writer's Choice feature provides examples from the works of well-known writers to illustrate good word choices, with brief comments to tell why particular words are effective.

Read the sentence about Peaches taken from a book by Walter Dean Myers and the comment that explains how *shuffled* helps to describe the character.

WRITER'S CHOICE

I watched as Peaches shuffled along the gate toward the entrance to the ball field.

—Walter Dean Myers, *Me, Mop, and the Moondance Kid*

Why *shuffled?* Peaches is a tramp. Walter Dean Myers uses *shuffled* to show that Peaches has very little energy, not even enough to pick his feet up off the ground.

- This particular Writer's Choice feature appears with the entry for *walk*. Why do you think *shuffled* is a better word choice for this sentence than *walked* would have been?

WORDS AT PLAY

• • • • • • • • • •

Limericks and other poems show the words and their synonyms used in amusing ways.

Enjoy the poem about an octopus.

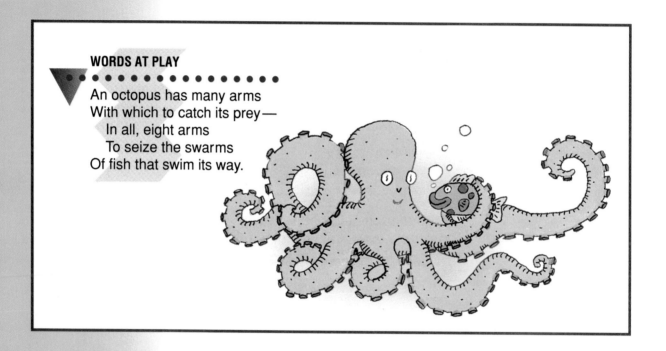

WORDS AT PLAY

• • • • • • • • • • • • • • • •

An octopus has many arms
With which to catch its prey—
   In all, eight arms
    To seize the swarms
Of fish that swim its way.

- This Words at Play feature appears with the entry for *catch* in this thesaurus. Find the word *catch* in the rhyme.

- Under *catch* you will find these synonyms: *trap, capture, seize, grab,* and *snatch.* Do you find any of these words in the rhyme?

WORD STORY

Have you ever wondered how words come into our language? There are many ways, and the history of a word can be surprising, even fascinating.

Brief Word Stories are included with many entries. *Vamoose*, a synonym under *leave*, is one example.

Vamoose means to leave very quickly and suddenly. It is slang. *When Jim started doing cannonballs, the fish vamoosed.*

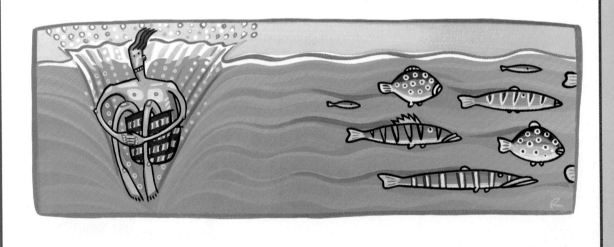

- From what language does *vamoose* come?
- What happened to the word when it came into English?

WRITING TIP

This feature gives helpful hints about how to make your writing livelier. Among the tips you will find suggestions for creating a mood, writing dialogue, and comparing things.

Writing Tips also help you to use a variety of words that are related to the same idea.

WRITING TIP: Make a Word Bank

A word bank is a list of words that share an idea. Suppose you want to write about circus clowns. You can start by making a word bank of all the words you think of when you think of clowns. Here are some words we thought of:

hilarious	ridiculous	comical	funny
silly	laughter	tricks	costume
grin	wig	shoes	gloves

When you plan what to write, your word bank will help you find ideas. When you are writing, your word bank will give you words, so you don't have to stop and think of them. This book can help you find words for the bank.

- What words in the word bank might be used in place of *comical?*

- What words might help you describe what a clown wears?

WORD WORKSHOP

Words such as *bad*, *good*, and *nice* tend to be used too much because they describe so many things. In the Word Workshop feature, examples show you exactly how writing can be improved with better word choices.

WORD WORKSHOP

The word *bad* is often overused. See what happens in the paragraphs below when we replace *bad* with more precise words. Some of the words that we have used come from the studies for **naughty, terrible,** and **wicked,** which the study for **bad** tells you to see.

Naughty
A Bad Bird?

awful
"I feel bad about this, Mrs. Simms," said the
an inferior
pet store owner. "It's a bad birdcage, all right. Too

bad that Peppy got out."

mischievous
"He does such bad things," Mrs. Simms com-

plained. "Like knocking over the birdseed. It was a
horrid   wicked
really bad mess. But I don't think he's a bad bird.
unsatisfactory
Maybe he wants to tell me he thinks the seed is bad,

and I should buy another kind."

"Not a bad idea," said the owner.

- Why do you think *awful* was chosen to replace *bad* in the first sentence?

- Why is *inferior* a better choice than *bad* in the next sentence?

WORD POOL
· · · · · · · ·

Some words that are not synonyms are related in other ways. They might be words for baby animals, such as *kitten*, *puppy*, *gosling*, and *duckling*, or words for kinds of breads, such as *bagel*, *biscuit*, *challah*, *cracker*, and *muffin*.

Use the Word Pool feature to enrich your vocabulary. The following example comes from the entry word *group*.

WORD POOL
· · · · · · · · · · · · · · · ·

Here are some special words for groups of animals.

a **brood** of chicks
a **covey** of quail
a **flock** of sheep
a **gaggle** of geese
a **herd** of cows or deer
a **litter** of kittens or puppies
a **pack** of wolves
a **pod** of seals or whales
a **pride** of lions
a **school** of dolphins or fish
a **swarm** of bees

- What is a group of wolves called?

- What is the name for a group of geese?

- You probably already knew some of these group words. Are there any that you didn't know before you read the list?

WORDS FROM WORDS
• • • • • • • • • • • • •

How are words added to, or combined, to form new words? This feature shows some of the ways.

Notice how many words are formed starting with the base word *soft*.

WORDS FROM WORDS
• • • • • • • • •

soft
softball
soft-boiled
soften
softener
softheaded
softhearted
soft-shelled
soft-spoken
software
softwood
softy

- The meaning of *soft* is "tender, not hard or stiff." Explain how the word *softball* is related to the meaning of *soft*.

- How are *softheaded* and *softhearted* related to *soft?*

P.S.
• • •

Did you know that P.S. stands for "postscript," which is something added to a letter or other piece of writing? A postscript usually gives some additional information.

Similarly, the P.S. feature provides additional information. For example, the following is included with *break*.

P.S.
• •

Break is used in phrases that have special meanings:

Break down can mean to stop working. *The bus broke down five blocks from school.*

Break in can mean to get something ready. *I need to break in my new shoes before I go for a long walk.*

Break into can mean to start suddenly. *Hector was so happy he broke into song.*

Break off can mean to stop suddenly. *The soccer game broke off when it suddenly started to rain.*

Break out can mean to begin, usually suddenly. *If war breaks out, my aunt's army unit will have to go.*

Break up can mean to end. *The softball game broke up when it got dark.*

• Which two phrases using *break* have special meanings about starting or beginning?

• Which two phrases using *break* have special meanings about stopping or ending?

Entries

A collection of entry words, their synonyms, and their antonyms

Adult

adjective

Adult means fully grown and developed. *The sixth graders cannot run as far as the adult runners.*

Grown-up means adult but is used especially in contrast to something childish. *April likes books for children more than stories for grown-up readers.*

Mature means fully grown and developed, especially mentally. *Jan is only eight, but mature for her age.*

Full-grown means fully grown and developed, especially physically. *By next year this tiny kitten will be a full-grown cat.*

ANTONYMS: childish, immature

P.S.

Sometimes words can be used in different ways. *Adult* and *grown-up* are also naming words, or nouns. See what we could have said:

> *The sixth graders cannot run as fast as the <u>adults</u>.*
>
> *April likes books for children more than stories for <u>grown-ups</u>.*

We chose to write about describing words, or adjectives, so that we could show you *mature* and *full-grown* too.

Afraid

adjective

Afraid means feeling fear. *Katie and I are afraid of snakes.*

Frightened means afraid. *The frightened deer leaped over the fence and ran away.*

Scared means the same as afraid but is less formal. *Levar is never scared of the dark.*

Alarmed means fearful and aware of danger. *We were all alarmed when we heard the explosion.*

Terrified means feeling great fear and dread. *The terrified children screamed when the tiger broke out of the cage.*

WORD STORY

Petrified comes from a Latin word meaning "turned into stone." That describes what fear can do to you.

Petrified can mean feeling fear so strong that it makes you unable to move or think. *When Tim first saw the rattlesnake he was petrified.*

SEE **fear** for words that mean the feeling of being afraid.

SEE **scare** for words that mean to make someone afraid.

SEE **terrifying** for words that mean scary.

ANTONYM: fearless

The **frightened** deer leaped over the fence and ran away.

Alone
adjective

Alone means being away from others. *Tiffany is twelve now, old enough to stay home alone.*

Solitary means alone, often because you choose to be. *Darryl went for a long, solitary walk.*

WORD STORY

• • • • • • • • • • • •

Isolated comes from a Latin word meaning "island." When you are isolated, you're cut off from others, like an island.

Isolated means alone and separated from others. *My mother grew up on an isolated farm, miles from the nearest town.*

Lone means alone. It is often used in stories and poems. *The ranchers wondered who the lone rider coming into Saddle Valley might be.*

Lonely means sad because of a need for company. You can be lonely because you are alone, but you can be alone and not feel lonely. In fact, sometimes you can feel lonely when you are with a lot of people, if you don't know them. *Luis didn't know anyone in his new class, and for the first week he felt lonely all day in school.*

By yourself means alone. *"Are you going to the playground by yourself, Tom?" asked his mother.*

WRITER'S CHOICE

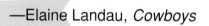

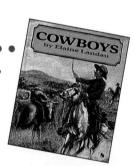

On a trail drive to the railroad station, the cowboy might be isolated from civilization for over three months at a time.

—Elaine Landau, *Cowboys*

Why *isolated?* Elaine Landau uses *isolated* to show that cowboys on a cattle drive were separated from other people for a long time.

Amount

noun

Amount means how much or how many. It is the figure you get when you add up all the things that you are measuring or counting. *Jackie spends only a small amount of her allowance on candy.*

Quantity means an amount. *Our school uses a large quantity of paper every week.*

Number means the figure you get when you count a group of people or things. *The number of horses in this riding show is six.*

Sum can mean the figure you get when you add a group of numbers together. *What is the sum of nine and three?*

Total means sum. *Veronica's cat has had a total of eighteen kittens.*

Veronica's cat has had a **total** of eighteen kittens.

Ancient
adjective

Ancient means very old. It is mostly used to describe things, but it can be used to describe people. *The ancient Mayan people built great temples and cities.*

Antique means of former times. It always describes things. *Dershon likes pictures of antique cars from the 1920s and 1930s.*

Old-fashioned means out of date in style, working, thinking, or behaving. *Old-fashioned tractors were pulled by mules.*

Prehistoric means from the time before there was written history. *At the museum, Clara saw prehistoric tools made out of rocks.*

The **ancient** Mayan people built great temples and cities.

Answer

noun

Answer means something that you say or write when someone asks a question. *When the teacher asks a question about science, Allie nearly always gives the answer first.*

Reply means an answer. It is a somewhat more formal word. It may suggest that the answer is a careful and complete one. *When Mrs. Ramirez asked the prices of new cars, the salesman gave her a reply with exact figures.*

Response means an answer. It is used about actions and about words. *The firefighters' response to the alarm was so quick that their truck arrived in five minutes.*

Retort means a quick, sharp answer. *When I asked Jack where he was going, his retort was, "None of your business!"*

ANTONYM: question

WRITER'S CHOICE

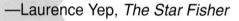

Turning, I could see Emily's mouth twisting open for some angry retort. Quickly I clapped my hand over her mouth.

—Laurence Yep, *The Star Fisher*

Why *retort?* Emily is a spunky little girl and a bully has insulted her family. Laurence Yep's use of *retort* indicates that Emily is about to return insult for insult when her sister stops her.

The Diaz family **argued** about whether to get a cat or a dog.

Argue

verb

Argue means to disagree strongly and give reasons for your point of view. *The Diaz family argued about whether to get a cat or a dog.*

Squabble means to argue childishly over small matters. *My little brother and sister squabble over who gets to sit in the front seat.*

Bicker means to squabble for a long period of time. *Jody and Mike bickered for months over who was the better cook.*

Quarrel means to argue noisily and angrily. *My parents are quarreling with our neighbors about the fence they put up.*

Feud means to quarrel fiercely for many years, often one group with another. *The two families feuded over the boundaries of their farms.*

Have it out is an idiom that means to argue until the question is settled. *My sister and I had it out about her riding my new bike without asking.*

SEE **fight** for words that mean to struggle.

Ascend

verb

Ascend means to go up or move up to the top of something. *Tom, Ramona, and Jake ascended the mountain.*

Climb means to go up, mainly by using hands and feet. *Scott will climb a ladder to take down the window screen.*

Mount can mean to get up on something. *Kyle mounted the horse and galloped down the trail.*

WORD STORY

Scale comes from a Latin word meaning "ladder" or "steps."

Scale can mean to climb up something. It suggests great effort. *The explorers scaled the high cliff and found a hidden lake below.*

SEE **rise** for more words that mean to go up.
ANTONYM: descend

Tom, Ramona, and Jake **ascended** the mountain.

WRITING TIP: The Way It Sounds

Sometimes it sounds odd to repeat a word:

"The *climbers climbed* the mountain."
"The climbers *mounted* the *mountain*."

So you can use another word, just to sound better:

"The climbers *ascended* the mountain."

Mrs. Ostrow **asked** the hotel clerk what arrangements
had been made for disabled people.

Ask

verb

Ask means to try to find out information through a question. *Mrs. Ostrow asked the hotel clerk what arrangements had been made for disabled people.*

Inquire means to ask in order to get detailed information. *Sasha inquired about the bus schedule at the ticket window.*

Quiz means to ask questions about what has been learned. *Our teacher will quiz us on today's spelling words.*

Question means to ask over and over again. *Ms. Garza questioned her class about what happened at recess.*

Interrogate means to ask someone many questions for a long time. *The lawyer interrogated the witness about the accident for two hours.*

ANTONYMS: answer, reply

Attack
verb

Attack means to start fighting someone or something with actions or words. *My dog attacks any stranger who enters our house. The newspaper attacked the plans for a new road.*

Assault means to attack suddenly, usually with weapons. *The kids down the block assaulted us with snowballs.*

Charge can mean to attack by a sudden rush. *The cat charged at the pigeons.*

Ambush means to attack from hiding. *The rustlers tried to ambush the sheriff, but he got away.*

Raid means to attack or enter suddenly and then leave. *The raccoons raid our garbage cans all the time.*

Gang up on is an idiom that means to attack in a group. *Chip's younger brothers ganged up on him in their pillow fight.*

SEE **fight** for words that mean to struggle.

The raccoons **raid** our garbage cans all the time.

One **clumsy** raccoon fell and dropped everything.

Awkward
adjective

Awkward means lacking grace, skill, or ease. *He is such an awkward dancer that he stepped on my toes twice. Joanne felt awkward on her first day in the new school.*

Clumsy means stiff and likely to bump into things or drop them. *The clumsy waiter tripped and spilled our salads.*

All thumbs is an idiom that means very clumsy, especially in working with your hands. *You shouldn't have asked someone who's all thumbs to help you put up that shelf.*

ANTONYM: graceful

WRITING TIP: Using Idioms

All thumbs is an interesting way of saying "clumsy." Imagine how clumsy people would be if their hands had five thumbs instead of one! A phrase like *all thumbs* is called an *idiom.* Idioms are phrases that have special meanings.

Another idiom is the phrase *lend a hand,* which means "to help." Would you want someone to lend a hand if that person were all thumbs?

Bad

adjective

Bad means not good or not as it ought to be. *Marty says the movie is bad because it bored him. Sandy's skateboard has a bad wheel.*

Unsatisfactory means not good enough. *The teacher asked Bob to rewrite his unsatisfactory book report.*

Poor can mean not good in quality. *The painters did a poor job, spilling a lot of paint on the floor.*

Inferior means worse than others or worse than it should be. *This inferior TV has never worked properly.*

SEE **naughty** for words that mean behaving badly.
SEE **terrible** for words that mean worse than bad.
SEE **wicked** for words that mean evil.
ANTONYMS: good, satisfactory

P.S.
• • • • • • • • • • • • • • • • • • • •

Some people use the word *bad* to mean very good.

She saved her baby-sitting money and bought herself some really bad hightop shoes.

This use of the word *bad* is slang.

Sandy's skateboard has a **bad** wheel.

The word *bad* is often overused. See what happens in the paragraphs below when we replace *bad* with more precise words. Some of the words that we have used come from the studies for **naughty, terrible,** and **wicked,** which the study for **bad** tells you to see.

Naughty
A ~~Bad~~ Bird?

awful
"I feel ~~bad~~ about this, Mrs. Simms," said the

an inferior
pet store owner. "It's ~~a bad~~ birdcage, all right. Too

bad that Peppy got out."

mischievous
"He does such ~~bad~~ things," Mrs. Simms com-

plained. "Like knocking over the birdseed. It was a

horrid   *wicked*
really ~~bad~~ mess. But I don't think he's a ~~bad~~ bird.

unsatisfactory
Maybe he wants to tell me he thinks the seed is ~~bad,~~

and I should buy another kind."

"Not a bad idea," said the owner.

Beautiful

adjective

Beautiful means delightful to see, hear, or think about. *In the fall the colors of some trees are beautiful.*

Pretty means pleasing to see or hear. It is often used to describe girls and women. *Cassie looks like her pretty mother.*

Handsome means pleasing to see. It is often used instead of *beautiful* or *pretty* to describe a man or boy. *That handsome cowboy rides a good-looking horse.*

Good-looking means handsome or pretty. *Rick's brother has dark hair and is very good-looking.*

Lovely means especially beautiful and fine. *It was a lovely evening, with a sky full of stars.*

Glamorous means fascinating and charming. *Monica thinks her favorite TV star is very glamorous.*

Gorgeous means very fancy or colorful. *The bride wore a gorgeous wedding dress.*

SEE **cute** for words that mean pleasing.
ANTONYM: ugly

That **handsome** cowboy rides a **good-looking** horse.

WRITING TIP: Overused Words

People often use the word *pretty* when another word would be better. Be careful not to overuse *pretty.* Try to think of the word that makes your idea clear. If you really like a picture, you could call it *beautiful* or *lovely,* instead of just pretty.

Pretty can also mean "fairly" or "somewhat": *He dances pretty well.* Try not to overuse this meaning too. Instead of *pretty cold,* you could say *chilly.* Instead of *pretty angry,* you could say *annoyed.*

The pull of the fish
made Leon's pole
bend.

Bend

verb

Bend means to change shape, or to make something change shape. *The pull of the fish made Leon's pole bend. Always bend your legs when you lift something heavy.*

Curve means to go out of a straight line, or to make something go out of a straight line. *Heather's lips curved in a smile.*

Twist can mean to bend. It suggests something that bends many times. *This electric cord is all twisted.*

Curl means to twist into many circles. *Fiona curled the strip of paper around her finger.*

Turn can mean to change direction by curving. *This bus will turn north at the next corner.*

Wind means to turn back and forth several times. *Raymond rides his bike on the winding road in the park.*

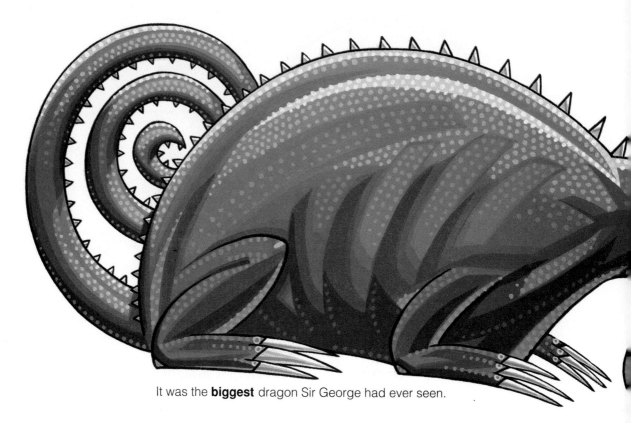

It was the **biggest** dragon Sir George had ever seen.

Big

adjective

Big means more than the usual size, number, or amount. *It was the biggest dragon Sir George had ever seen.*

Large means big. It often describes the space or amount of something. *The giant needed a very large house to live in. Now that Ivor is away from home, we have a large phone bill.*

Great means large and out of the ordinary. *The great mountain peaks rose above us and made us feel small.*

Bulky means big and awkward because of its size. *It was hard to get the bulky package through the narrow door.*

SEE **huge** for words that mean bigger than big.
ANTONYMS: little, small

Brave

adjective

Brave means showing no fear of danger. *The brave girl rescued her sister from the fire.*

Courageous means brave and strong in spirit. A courageous person does what is right even when it is hard or dangerous. *It was courageous of Brad to tell me that he spilled grape juice on my new sweater.*

Bold means willing and eager to face danger and take risks. *It's a movie about a bold girl with limited hearing who learns to fly a plane.*

Daring means bold. *Kikuko's favorites were the daring women and men in the trapeze act.*

Heroic means very brave and noble. Heroic people often put themselves in danger to help others. *A heroic lifeguard saved my brother from drowning.*

Gallant means fearless and eager to show bravery. It is a formal word. *Gallant Sir George fought the fierce dragon.*

Valiant means very brave in facing difficulty or trying to reach a goal. *We made a valiant effort but lost the game to the stronger team.*

ANTONYM: cowardly

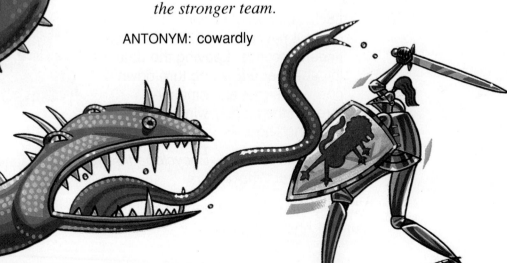

Gallant Sir George fought the fierce dragon.

Break

verb

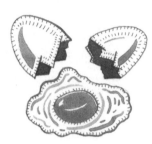

The egg fell and **broke** in two.

Break means to come apart suddenly or to force something to come apart. *The egg fell and broke in two. Mom broke the stick over her knee.*

Crack means to break, but not into pieces. *The stone cracked the window, but the glass did not fall out.*

Shatter means to break into many pieces. *The cup shattered when it hit the floor.*

Smash means to break something by great force. *A driver who hits a tree will smash the car.*

Split means to break or to divide into parts. *We split several logs into firewood for the fireplace. Kyle split his snack with Thalia.*

Fracture means to crack hard things, such as bones. *If you fall out of a tree, you may fracture your leg.*

SEE **destroy** for words that mean to break something to bits.
SEE **harm** for words that mean to break something a little bit.

WRITER'S CHOICE

Lucia Ankram of London, England, drove a new car in 1975—for about fifteen seconds. Leaving the dealer's lot, she made a wrong turn down a one-way street and smashed through the display window of a dry-cleaning shop.

—Donald J. Sobol, *Encyclopedia Brown's Book of Wacky Cars*

Why *smashed*? Donald Sobol's use of *smashed* suggests the sound of breaking glass.

Break is used in phrases that have special meanings:

Break down can mean to stop working. *The bus broke down five blocks from school.*

Break in can mean to get something ready. *I need to break in my new shoes before I go for a long walk.*

Break into can mean to start suddenly. *Hector was so happy he broke into song.*

Break off can mean to stop suddenly. *The soccer game broke off when it suddenly started to rain.*

Break out can mean to begin, usually suddenly. *If war breaks out, my aunt's army unit will have to go.*

Break up can mean to end. *The softball game broke up when it got dark.*

The soccer game **broke off** when it suddenly started to rain.

Lupe's **radiant** smile showed how happy she was.

Bright

adjective

▼ **WORD POOL**
• • • • • • • • • •
There are many words for what bright light can do. These words are not synonyms, but they are related words.

flicker
gleam
glitter
shimmer
sparkle
twinkle

Bright means giving a lot of light. *The bright sun caused Kara to blink.*

Shiny means reflecting a lot of light. *The shiny pan showed that Meimei had scrubbed it clean.*

Brilliant means very bright. *The brilliant outdoor lights let us play ball after dark.*

Radiant means seeming full of light. *Lupe's radiant smile showed how happy she was.*

Sunny means bright with sunshine. *Such a sunny place is perfect for a garden.*

Glowing means bright with a warm soft light. *Glowing candles lit the room.*

Dazzling means bright enough to hurt the eyes. *Sunlight on snow is dazzling.*

Glaring means dazzling. *Amy turned her eyes away from the glaring car headlights.*

ANTONYMS: dark, dim

Careless

adjective

WORDS FROM WORDS
• • • • • • • • • •

care
carefree
careful
caregiver
careless
carelessly
carelessness
caring
uncaring

Careless means not careful. *Sonia was careless about shutting all the windows, and the curtains got soaked when it rained.*

Thoughtless means not thinking before doing something. *It was thoughtless of Julian to mention Lateisha's party, since Miriam wasn't invited.*

Inconsiderate means thoughtless of other people's feelings. *Our inconsiderate neighbors make a lot of noise.*

Reckless means not thinking about possible danger. *The squirrels seem reckless, but they never fall from the trees.*

ANTONYMS: careful, cautious, watchful

Our **inconsiderate** neighbors make a lot of noise.

Carry

verb

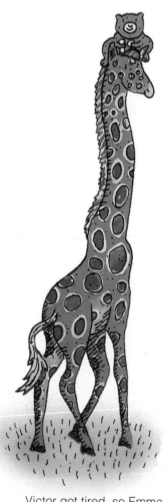

Victor got tired, so Emma **carried** him part of the way.

Carry means to hold something while you move from one place to another. *"Please help me carry the mattress up to the attic,"* said Mr. Tucker. *Victor got tired, so Emma carried him part of the way.*

Transport means to carry something in a ship, plane, car, truck, train, or other vehicle. *Trains no longer transport as many passengers as they once did.*

Bear means to carry something, often something heavy. *"Will that small bike bear your weight?" asked Jolene.*

Pack can mean to carry. *If you're going for a long walk, you had better pack a sandwich.*

Haul means to carry or drag. *The baby still hauls her blanket everywhere she goes.*

SEE **send** for words that mean to make something go somewhere.

▼ **P.S.**
• •

Carry is used in phrases that have special meanings:

Carry away means to make someone have strong feelings. *Martina was so angry that she got carried away and yelled at her friend.*

Carry back means to make someone remember something. *That song carries me back to when I was in the navy.*

Carry on can mean to misbehave. *"Will you stop all that carrying on and go to sleep!" said Tom's mother.*

Carry out means to get something done. *Our teacher carried out his promise of a class trip to the zoo.*

boat

wheelbarrow

WORD POOL

There are many ways to transport people and things from one place to another. We call these "means of transportation." These words are not synonyms, but they name related things. You can probably think of some we didn't list.

airplane
barge
bicycle
boat
bus
car
cart
dogsled
freight train
handcart
motorcycle
pickup truck
shopping cart
train
truck
wagon
wheelbarrow

dogsled

truck

train

bicycle

barge

carry 45

An octopus has many arms
With which to catch its prey—
  In all, eight arms
   To seize the swarms
Of fish that swim its way.

Catch

verb

Catch means to get hold of someone or something that is moving. *The police tried to catch the man who took the money and ran. Let's catch some fish for dinner.*

Trap means to catch and keep hold of an animal or a person. *Workers at the zoo spent all day trying to trap the escaped leopard.*

Capture means to take by force. *The pirates captured the treasure ship.*

Seize means to take suddenly and by force. *King Richard's soldiers seized the enemy camp and soon won the battle.*

Grab means to seize, especially by hand. *Pablo grabbed the cat before it got out the door.*

Snatch means to grab. *Demaris's hat blew off, but she snatched it out of the air.*

Cheat

verb

Cheat means to do something dishonest while hoping others won't notice. *Susan never cheats at games, and she won't play with anyone else who does.*

Trick means to cheat by misleading or fooling someone. *The villain tricked the cowboy by selling him a good horse and then changing it for another horse that wasn't as good.*

Deceive means to make someone believe something that isn't true. *When the fish hide in the seaweed, their stripes deceive enemies into thinking the fish aren't there.*

Swindle means to cheat someone, usually out of money. *A dishonest roofer swindled the church out of thousands of dollars.*

When the fish hide in the seaweed, their stripes **deceive** enemies into thinking the fish aren't there.

Choose

verb

Choose means to decide to take something. *Bob always chooses the yellow cup.*

Pick means to choose from many things just what you want. *When the two teams chose sides, each captain tried to pick the best players.*

Select means to choose from many things after thinking carefully. *It was time for Kim to select which dog would lead the team in the dogsled race.*

Elect means to choose one person from others by voting. *The fourth grade will elect class officers today.*

Pick out means to choose with extra care. *I picked out a sweater in my favorite shade of blue.*

It was time for Kim to **select** which dog would lead the team in the dogsled race.

Cold

adjective

Cold means having or feeling no warmth. *Ice cream is cold. Cold and clear, it was a beautiful day for the dogsled race.*

Cool means somewhat cold, in a pleasant way. *The weather was cool and comfortable.*

Chilly means unpleasantly cold. *It is too chilly to go swimming this morning.*

Frosty means cold enough to see your breath. *It was a frosty morning, so we wore warm clothing.*

Freezing means so cold that people are very uncomfortable. *"Shut the door, please; it's freezing outside," said Mrs. Shimkus.*

Icy means extremely cold, like ice. *An icy wind blew from the lake.*

ANTONYMS: hot, warm

Cold and clear, it was a beautiful day for the dogsled race.

 P.S.

● ●

People sometimes use "cold" words to describe feelings. These words can mean "unfriendly." They can also mean "angry, in a stiff, proud way."

She gave me a cold greeting and walked on down the hall.

He has been cool to me since I made that joke about him.

"Don't try to apologize," was my chilly reply.

The enemies met in frosty silence.

Their faces showed freezing rage and icy scorn.

Come

verb

Come means to get to a place. *The bus hasn't come yet, and I'm going to be late for school.*

Arrive means to get to a place, usually after a trip of some length. *Everyone was delighted when Cousin Hester arrived from Atlanta.*

Reach means to get to a place, often after a lot of work. *After traveling all day, Gerry reached his aunt's house.*

Show up means to come somewhere. It suggests a strong chance of not coming there. *I didn't think she would attend my party, but she showed up at the last moment.*

ANTONYMS: go away, leave

P.S.

Come is used in phrases that have special meanings:

Come down with means to catch an illness. *After I got so wet and tired, I came down with a cold.*

Come on means to start, please. *"Come on, everybody's waiting for you!" shouted Timmy eagerly.*

Come up with means to think of something. *Nikki came up with an idea that pleased the whole family.*

How come means why. *"How come you went to the movies and didn't tell me?" demanded my sister.*

Everyone was delighted when Cousin Hester **arrived** from Atlanta.

Belinda always sits in the same **comfortable** chair to read.

Comfortable

adjective

Comfortable means giving or feeling comfort and pleasure. *Belinda always sits in the same comfortable chair to read.*

Cozy means comfortable, warm, and giving or feeling friendly happiness. *The brightly colored pillows made the room cheerful and cozy.*

Snug means comfortable and sheltered, usually in a small space. *The sleeping bag kept Anna warm and snug during the cold night.*

Easy can mean comfortable and free from care or worry. *My uncle's easy manner makes us feel at home when we stay with him.*

ANTONYM: uncomfortable

"It's my turn!" **squawked** Sharon.

Complain

verb

Complain means to say that you are unhappy about something that is wrong. *"This store never has any good candy,"* *Teresa complained.*

Grumble means to complain in a growling, angry way. *Errol is grumbling about not getting to pitch.*

Whine can mean to complain in a sad voice about unimportant things. *When my baby sister is tired, she whines about everything.*

Gripe means to complain in a continuous, annoying way. *"If you don't stop griping, you won't get any dessert at all,"* *said Al's mother.*

Squawk can mean to complain loudly. This use is slang. *"It's my turn!" squawked Sharon.*

Cross

adjective

Cross means in a bad mood. *Sheila is cross today because she lost her favorite hat.*

Cranky and **crabby** mean becoming angry easily and grumbling about everything. *The cranky child threw down his toys and wouldn't play with them. He was crabby because he needed his nap.*

Grumpy and **grouchy** mean bad-tempered and complaining. *The reason I'm grumpy is that I have a bad headache, so leave me alone. When the headache stops, I won't be grouchy anymore.*

WORD STORY

Ornery is a shortened American form of *ordinary*. Is it ordinary for people to be ornery?

Ornery means always bad-tempered and hard to get along with. *The ornery woman who works in the grocery store has no friends.*

SEE **anger** for words that mean the feeling when you lose your temper.
SEE **mad** for words that mean angry.
ANTONYM: cheerful

WRITER'S CHOICE

A child grump, though, was something Fiona had never run into before. She had known kids who were irritable now and then, but Barbara was just grumpy by nature, grumpy at everybody, and grumpy for no particular reason.

—Beverly Keller, *Only Fiona*

Why *grumpy?* Beverly Keller uses *grumpy* because Barbara is not just in a bad mood. She is bad-tempered and complaining all the time.

Crowd

noun

Crowd means a large group of people together. *How will we ever find Frank and his dog in this huge crowd?*

Mob means a crowd, especially a noisy and violent one. *Police kept the angry mob from causing damage.*

Flock can mean crowd. *A flock of kids runs onto the playground when recess begins.*

Swarm can mean a crowd moving together. *During the sale, a swarm of shoppers filled the store.*

How will we ever find Frank and his dog in this huge **crowd?**

Cut
verb

Cut means to divide or to remove with something sharp. *"Will you cut the cake?" Mother asked Aunt Bella. George cut the ribbon from the package.*

Cut is also used in phrases that have special meanings. Each of these phrases has it own set of synonyms.

cut down

Cut down means to make something fall by cutting it. *At the end of the summer, Grandfather cuts down his bean plants.*

Chop down means to cut down. *The workers chopped down the dead tree in the park.*

cut off

Cut off means to remove by cutting. *Mom made my old jeans into shorts by cutting off the bottoms.*

Trim means to cut off parts that are not needed or not neat. *The barber trims my hair every two months.*

Shave means to cut off hair with a razor. *Mr. Pavic shaves with an electric razor.*

Snip means to cut something off with small, quick strokes. *Jay snipped a thread that was hanging from his sleeve.*

Shear means to remove something, especially wool, using shears, scissors, or clippers. *Ranchers shear their sheep in the spring.*

Ranchers **shear** their sheep in the spring.

cut out	**Cut out** means to remove something by cutting all the way around it. *"Do people still cut out paper dolls?" asked Jack.*

Clip can mean to cut something out of a magazine or newspaper. *Sara clipped a picture from the magazine to illustrate her report.*

cut up	**Cut up** means to divide by cutting. *"Please cut up the carrots, Jim," said Mrs. Schultz. "I'll do the coleslaw."*

Carve and **slice** mean to cut something up by moving a knife back and forth through it. *Jane carved the turkey. Then she sliced some bread.*

Split means to cut up, usually from end to end. *Ramón split the loaf of Italian bread and spread butter and garlic powder on it.*

Saw means to cut up with short back-and-forth strokes. *Ceretha sawed at the rope with a knife.*

Chop means to cut something up by hitting it with a sharp tool. *The man used an ax to chop wood for the fire.*

P.S.
● ●

These phrases have other meanings, too:

Cut down can mean to take less or use less of something. *My dentist says to cut down on sugar.*

Cut off can mean to stop or block. *Traffic was cut off by the fire at the corner store.*

Cut out can mean to stop doing something. *Mr. Thomas told the boys to cut out the arguing.*

Cut up can mean to hurt someone's feelings. *He was badly cut up by her unfriendliness.*

Cute

adjective

WORD POOL

Baby animals are cute. Some of them have special names. The kind of animal is shown in parentheses.

calf (cow)
chick (chicken)
cub (bear, lion, wolf)
duckling (duck)
fawn (deer)
foal (horse)
gosling (goose)
kid (goat)
kitten (cat)
lamb (sheep)
piglet (pig)
puppy (dog)

Cute means pleasing or good-looking. It is commonly used to show liking and approval. *Tim's little brother is cute. What a cute dress Nina is wearing. The puppies were all so cute it was hard to decide which one to pick.*

Attractive means pleasing to look at and interesting. *Vivien's room is very attractive. That attractive young man is my neighbor.*

Appealing means attractive and enjoyable. *Miguel has a good sense of humor and is very appealing.*

Amusing means pleasantly entertaining and interesting. *I like spending time with Cindy because she is amusing.*

Charming means pleasant and fascinating. *"I enjoyed meeting your charming cousin, Leila," said Mrs. Farrell.*

SEE **beautiful** for words that mean very good to see.
SEE **nice** for words that mean pleasant.

cub

fawn

puppy

lamb

piglet

Damp

adjective

WORD STORY

Damp comes from an old Dutch or German word meaning "water in the air," like mist or fog.

Damp means slightly wet, often in an unpleasant way. *Angela hurried to get out of her damp bathing suit.*

Moist means slightly wet, often in a pleasant way. *Belinda prefers a moist cake to a dry one.*

Humid means having a lot of moisture in the air. *Today it is 90 degrees and very humid.*

Clammy means cold and damp. *Jackie shivered in the dark, clammy basement.*

SEE **wet** for words that mean wetter than damp.

WRITING TIP: Creating a Mood

Sometimes when you write you want to create a mood—a special feeling. How are the moods of these two sentences different?

We plodded homeward through the clammy evening mists.

We strolled homeward through the moist evening air.

The mood of the first sentence is weary and unpleasant. The mood of the second sentence is cheerful and relaxed. Choosing words carefully is a way to create moods in your writing.

Climbing mountains can be **dangerous.**

Dangerous
adjective

Dangerous means likely to cause injury or harm. *Climbing mountains can be dangerous.*

Risky means involving a chance of injury or harm. *It is risky to ride in a car without buckling your seat belt.*

Unsafe means probably dangerous. *The city cut down the dead tree because it was unsafe.*

Hazardous means full of danger. *The mountain climbers studied the hazardous cliff.*

Perilous means dangerous. *Two Ponies will set out tomorrow on his perilous journey.*

ANTONYMS: harmless, safe

Descend
verb

Descend means to come down. *Holly used the stairs to descend from the top of the monument.*

Drop can mean to descend. *A golden leaf dropped onto Kerrie's head.*

Land can mean to come down from the sky. *Airplanes land one after another at this busy airport.*

Sink means to descend slowly or gradually. *The afternoon sun sinks toward the western hills.*

Take a nosedive is an idiom that means to descend quickly at a steep angle, front first. *In the video game, the rocket ship took a nosedive toward the planet's surface.*

SEE **fall** for words that mean to come down fast.
ANTONYMS: ascend, rise

WORDS AT PLAY

He thought he saw a Banker's Clerk
    Descending from the bus.
He looked again, and found it was
    A Hippopotamus.
"If this should stay to dine," he said,
"There won't be much for us!"

— Lewis Carroll

Destroy
verb

Destroy means to put an end to something, often by breaking or pulling it to pieces. *We destroyed our sand castle before the ocean waves could wash it away.*

Demolish means to smash or pull something to pieces. *A bulldozer can demolish brick walls.*

Wreck means to damage badly or completely. *Two cars were wrecked in the accident.*

Ruin means to make something worthless or useless. *Bugs that eat leaves can ruin a garden.*

Spoil means to ruin. *The paint spilled on Tyler's drawing and spoiled it.*

Annihilate means to destroy completely. *Three trailers were annihilated by the tornado.*

Tear down means to demolish. *After part of their garage burned, the Singhs tore down the rest and built a new one.*

SEE **break** for words that mean to come apart or knock apart.
SEE **harm** for words that mean to break something a bit.
ANTONYMS: create, make

We **destroyed** our sand castle before the ocean waves could wash it away.

This photograph is **blurred** because the runners were moving so fast.

Dim
adjective

Dim means not clearly seen, heard, or understood. *The light is too dim for reading. Most people have only a dim idea of how television works.*

Unclear means hard to understand. *Tanya's directions were unclear, and we got lost.*

WORD STORY

Vague comes from a Latin word meaning "wandering." If you wander, you have no exact idea where to go.

Vague means not exact or precise. *I have a vague memory of his face, but I forget his name.*

Blurred means having vague outlines or edges. *This photograph is blurred because the runners were moving so fast.*

Fuzzy can mean blurred. *Now that I have glasses, things no longer look fuzzy.*

Faint means very dim and hardly noticeable. *The music was so faint Rosella could hardly hear it.*

ANTONYMS: bright, clear

Dirty
adjective

Dirty means not clean. *Teesha's clothes got dirty when she played in the park.*

Filthy and **grimy** mean extremely dirty. *My hands got filthy from those grimy boards.*

Soiled means made dirty. It is often used to describe clothes. *Ron's mother would not let him wear the soiled shirt.*

Foul can mean so dirty that it is disgusting. *We got the doll out of the garbage, but it was too foul to keep.*

Smudged means marked with streaks of dirt. *The mirror was smudged where the twins had touched it with their dirty hands.*

Stained means marked with a color that will not wash out. *The tablecloth is stained with tea.*

Dingy means dirty-looking from long use. *Lori didn't want to sleep in the dingy old tent.*

ANTONYM: clean

WORD STORY

Soiled comes from a Latin word meaning "pig." Pigs like to roll in mud because it helps them to stay cool.

WRITER'S CHOICE

She looked up and examined the white clouds that dragged along in the vast blue sky. They all had dusty purple undersides like the smudged bottoms of dirty feet.

—Laurie Lawlor, *Addie's Dakota Winter*

Why *smudged*? Addie is a farm girl who goes barefoot a lot. Laurie Lawlor uses *smudged* to describe the look of feet streaked with dirt.

Eric **did** a nice job pulling weeds out of the garden.

Do
verb

Do means to take a piece of work and finish it. *Eric did a nice job pulling weeds out of the garden.*

Perform means to do something that needs practice, usually in public. *The acrobats perform thrilling stunts on the high wire.*

Accomplish means to do something that needs time and effort. *"Did you accomplish all those tasks in one day?" asked Ms. Wong.*

Achieve means to succeed in doing something important and difficult. *Gina studied hard and achieved a very high mark on her final exam.*

Carry out means to do. *The teachers' aides and the school janitors have different jobs to carry out.*

SEE **end** for words that mean to finish completely.

P.S.
• •

People use the word *do* with other action words when they want to show that they really mean something:

"I do believe in spooks," said the Cowardly Lion.

"I did go to the store, but they are out of turnips," declared Jess.

"Chuck does like you, but he's too shy to say so," Mrs. Schmidt assured Keith.

The diver looked at the sharks with **mistrust.**

Doubt

noun

Doubt means a feeling of not believing something or not being sure. *He listened with doubt to their excuses. Mrs. Twofeathers has doubts about whether to buy a new car.*

Uncertainty means a feeling of not being sure of someone or something. *Uncertainty about the weather caused them to cancel the picnic.*

WORD STORY

• • • • • • • • • • • •

Suspicion comes from a Latin word meaning "to look under." A feeling of suspicion makes you want to "look under" something to see what's really going on.

Suspicion means a feeling of not trusting someone. This word is often used in connection with a crime or bad deed. *Henry finished the mystery and learned that his suspicion of the cook was correct.*

Mistrust means suspicion or lack of trust. *The diver looked at the sharks with mistrust.*

Distrust means strong suspicion or a serious lack of trust. *Officer Nokomo saw the woman hide something, so he watched her with distrust.*

ANTONYMS: belief, certainty

Dull
adjective

Dull means not interesting. *She told a dull story in which nothing happened.*

Uninteresting means too common and ordinary to hold your interest. *With only three players the game was pretty uninteresting.*

Boring means so dull that it makes you unhappy. *When something is boring, five minutes can seem like half an hour.*

Tiresome means dull and making you tired. *Washing clothes by hand must be tiresome.*

Monotonous means boring and always the same. *The scenery was monotonous when we drove across the empty prairie.*

ANTONYM: interesting

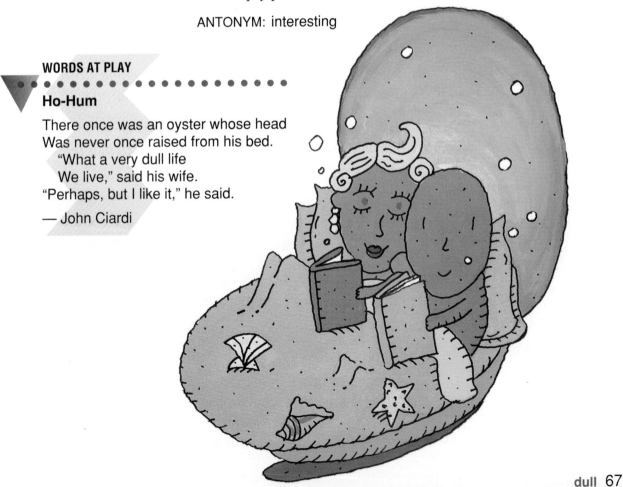

Eager
adjective

Eager means wanting something very much or looking forward to doing it. *Annette has practiced her song for three days and now is eager to sing it.*

Impatient can mean eager and unwilling to wait for something. *Ramón is impatient to learn sign language so he can talk with the girl who moved in next door.*

Enthusiastic means eager and excited. *The enthusiastic scouts sang loudly as they marched in the parade.*

Gung-ho means extremely enthusiastic. It is an informal word. *The girls on this team are so gung-ho that they practice every night.*

WRITING TIP: Remember Your Reader

When you write, it is important to keep your reader in mind. If you remember who will read your writing, that will help you choose the right word. What kind of reader does the writer have in mind for each of these sentences?

Recently I have become enthusiastic about skateboarding.

I've gotten really gung-ho about skateboarding lately.

The first sentence might be part of a report written for a teacher. The second might come from a letter to a friend. Both *enthusiastic* and *gung-ho* mean "eager." Which word you choose depends on who your reader is.

Easy
adjective

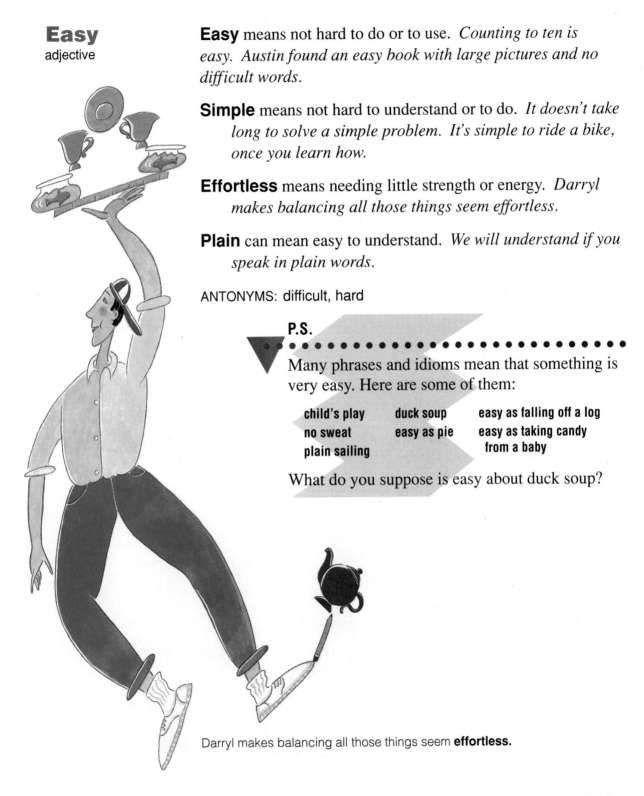

Easy means not hard to do or to use. *Counting to ten is easy. Austin found an easy book with large pictures and no difficult words.*

Simple means not hard to understand or to do. *It doesn't take long to solve a simple problem. It's simple to ride a bike, once you learn how.*

Effortless means needing little strength or energy. *Darryl makes balancing all those things seem effortless.*

Plain can mean easy to understand. *We will understand if you speak in plain words.*

ANTONYMS: difficult, hard

P.S.

Many phrases and idioms mean that something is very easy. Here are some of them:

child's play   duck soup   easy as falling off a log

no sweat   easy as pie   easy as taking candy from a baby

plain sailing

What do you suppose is easy about duck soup?

Darryl makes balancing all those things seem **effortless.**

Eat

verb

WORD POOL

Here are more words about eating. These are not synonyms, but they are related words. Use your dictionary to find their meanings.

bite
chew
chomp
feast
gnaw
gulp
munch
swallow
taste
wolf down

Eat means to put food in the mouth and swallow. *We ate lunch outside yesterday. Tawana doesn't like to eat soup on hot days.*

Consume can mean to use up an amount of food. *The farm animals consume large amounts of food every morning.*

Devour means to eat hungrily or greedily. *The hungry lion devoured the meat. Bert devoured three sandwiches.*

Feed can mean to eat. It is used mostly for animals. *Horses feed on hay and grain.*

Graze means to eat grass. *In summer, flocks of sheep graze on the mountainside.*

Dine means to eat dinner. *The truck drivers stopped to dine at Maud's Restaurant.*

Snack means to eat between meals. *Angela likes to snack on fruit when she gets home from school.*

Nibble means to eat in small bites. *My little sister is nibbling a cracker.*

Gobble means to eat quickly, in large bites or gulps. *Jasmine's father told his children not to gobble their food.*

The farm animals **consume** large amounts of food every morning.

All over the world, there are different kinds of bread to eat. You can find all of the breads listed here in any big city in the United States, and many of them are in every supermarket. How many of these have you eaten?

bagel
baguette
bialy
biscuit
bun
challah
chapati
cornbread
cracker
croissant
crumpet
dumpling
English muffin
matzo
muffin
papadam
pita
popover
roll
scone
tortilla

Edge
noun

Edge means the line or place where something ends. *A square piece of paper has four edges. We live on the edge of the city.*

Margin means an area next to an edge. *Leave wide margins when you write on a sheet of paper.*

Rim means the edge of something round. *Yoko's shot hit the rim of the basket but didn't fall in.*

Border means an edge of a place or the area along the edge. *Texas forms part of the United States border with Mexico.*

Boundary means a border. *The used-car lot has a high fence along its boundaries.*

WORDS AT PLAY
. . . .

The Sad Story of a Little Boy Who Cried

Our dear little Jack was ever so good.
   Then he decided to cry all he could.
He cried all day and he cried all night,
   He cried in the morning and at twilight;
He cried till his voice was as hoarse as a crow,
   And his mouth grew as large as a great big O.
It grew at the bottom and grew at the top;
   It grew till we thought it would never stop.
Each day his mouth grew wider and taller
   And his dear little self grew thinner and smaller.
At last his mouth grew so big that—alack!—
   It was only a mouth with a border of Jack.

Nothing but weeds grew in the **vacant** lot.

Empty
adjective

Empty means with nothing in it. *It's hard to study on an empty stomach. The Wangs moved away, and now their house is empty.*

Vacant means with nothing on it or in it. It is used mostly to describe places. *Nothing but weeds grew in the vacant lot.*

Blank means with nothing on it. It is used mostly to describe flat things. *Mr. Dawkins gave each student a blank piece of paper.*

Hollow means empty inside. *Pak climbed into the hollow tree trunk.*

ANTONYM: full

End

verb

Pete **completed** the statue in time to enter it in the art show.

End means to come to the last part of something or to bring it to its last part. *The game ended in a tie. Yellow Bird's brother ended his performance with a somersault.*

Finish and **complete** mean to end what you started to do. These words suggest that you have done everything necessary. *Jenny finished painting the picture before lunchtime. Pete completed the statue in time to enter it in the art show.*

Conclude is a formal word that means to end. *Mr. Joyner concluded the assembly by awarding the Lopez Prize for the best work of art.*

Close can mean to bring something to an end. *The school chorus closed the talent show by singing "America the Beautiful."*

SEE **last** for words that mean final.
SEE **stop** for words that mean to make something end.
ANTONYMS: begin, start

WRITING TIP: Using a Dictionary

Your thesaurus lists different words that share a meaning. Sometimes you may want to know different meanings of one word. For example, does *close* mean the same thing in the following sentences?

The clown closed her act by juggling hats.

Please close the door on your way out.

To discover the different meanings that one word can have, you need to use a dictionary. The dictionary also helps you to spell and say words correctly.

Fair
adjective

Fair means right and not favoring one person over another. *It is fair for every player to have a turn.*

Just means fair, based upon rules or laws. *The judge's decision was popular because it was just.*

Unbiased means trying to be completely fair. *Please find an unbiased person to settle your argument.*

Impartial means not favoring one person or one side over another. *The umpire must be impartial and say exactly what happened.*

ANTONYM: unfair

The umpire must be **impartial** and say exactly what happened.

Fall

verb

Fall means to come down suddenly, often out of control. *When Becky fell on the rocks, she hurt her knee.*

Drop means to fall or to let something fall. *Some money dropped out of the hole in my pocket.*

WORD STORY

Tumble comes from an old English word meaning "to dance about." They must have done strange dances in the old days.

Tumble means to fall in a helpless way. *Maria tumbled into the swimming pool.*

Topple means to fall as a result of becoming unsteady. *If you stack boxes too high, they will topple.*

Collapse means to fall down or apart. *The empty old barn finally collapsed.*

Keel over can mean to fall over suddenly, usually unconscious. *After standing a long time in the hot sun, several people keeled over in the grass.*

SEE **descend** for more words that mean to come down.
ANTONYM: rise

P.S.

Fall is used in phrases that have special meanings:

Fall back on means to rely on someone or something when others fail. *If I can't get a summer job in the supermarket, I'll fall back on baby-sitting.*

Fall for is an informal phrase that means to be fooled by something. *I really fell for her story about knowing the governor.*

Fall through means to fail. *Our picnic plans fell through when it rained.*

The empty old barn finally **collapsed.**

The animals rushed out of the collapsing barn in **fear.**

Fear
noun

WORD STORY

Alarm comes from Italian words meaning "to arms." This was a warning to soldiers to grab their weapons.

Fear means the feeling of being scared. *The animals rushed out of the collapsing barn in fear.*

Fright means sudden fear. *Waking up to the sound of a siren gave me a terrible fright.*

Alarm means fright caused by danger. *The rabbit hopped away in alarm when we got too close to it.*

Dread means great fear of something that may happen. *Nicola watched with dread as the two planes flew toward each other.*

Terror means very great fear. *People in the burning building shouted in terror.*

Horror means terror and a creepy feeling. *The ghost story filled us with horror.*

SEE **afraid** for words that mean having fear.
SEE **scare** for words that mean to make someone afraid.
SEE **terrifying** for words that mean scary.
ANTONYMS: bravery, courage

Fight
verb

Fight means to oppose someone or something with actions or words. *The puppies fight a lot, but they never hurt each other. If I ask to stay up late, Mom will fight me over it.*

Struggle means to fight with difficulty. *Joshua struggled to get his stubborn calf back inside the gate.*

Battle means to fight for a period of time. *Teresa's team battled all summer for first place.*

Combat means to fight something strongly. *Our class combats pollution by helping at the recycling center.*

War means to fight strongly for a long time. *After years of warring with the British, Americans won their independence.*

SEE **argue** for words that mean to fight with words.
SEE **attack** for words that mean to start a fight.

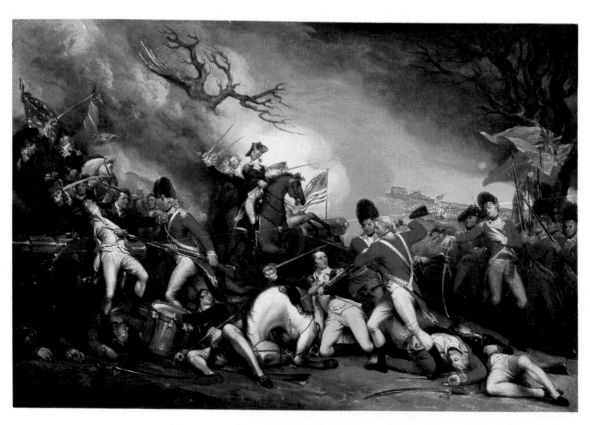

After years of **warring** with the British, Americans won their independence.

Find
verb

Bonnie **discovered** some baby birds in a nest.

Find means to come upon something. *"Please help me find my book,"* said Roberta. *Sandy found a dollar on the street.*

Discover means to find something that has not been known or that has been hidden. *Bonnie discovered some baby birds in a nest.*

Locate can mean to find the position of something. *The wheelchair ramp was easy to locate.*

Spot can mean to locate. *Raymond spotted Monkey Island on the zoo map.*

Dig up can mean to look for and find something. *My cousin dug up an old hat to wear on Halloween.*

ANTONYMS: lose, misplace

WRITER'S CHOICE

DDT, once hailed as a "miracle" destroyer of insect pests, had just been banned in Canada because scientists had discovered that it greatly harmed the environment.

—Lisa Yount, *Black Scientists*

Why *discovered?* Lisa Yount uses *discovered* because DDT had been harming the environment all along, but for years the problems were not known.

Many birds **flew** up together.

Fly
verb

Fly means to move through the air by using wings. *Many birds flew up together.*

Wing can mean to fly. It is used mostly about living things. *Some butterflies may wing thousands of miles in a year.*

Flap can mean to fly with large movements of the wings. *The pigeons flap loudly from the sidewalk to the roof.*

Flutter can mean to move the wings quickly but not strongly. *Our parakeet Amigo got out of his cage and fluttered around the room.*

SEE **rise** for words that mean to go up.

Friend
noun

Friend means someone you like and who likes you. *When it is hot, my friends and I stand in the water from the hose.*

Comrade means a friend who shares what you are doing. *The boys in the scout troop are comrades.*

Playmate means a person you play with often. *Tara and Jewel have been playmates since kindergarten.*

Companion means a close friend who goes along. *Ursula's cousins were her companions all through last summer's camping trip.*

Pal means a close friend. *Esteban wants to invite a pal for dinner on Friday.*

Amigo means a close friend who understands you well. *Danny is a real amigo, and I can tell him anything.*

Buddy is an informal word that means a close friend. *Norman's buddy waited for him at the corner.*

ANTONYM: enemy

When it is hot, my **friends** and I stand in the water from the hose.

Full
adjective

Full means holding as much as possible. *Parents' Day was a full day at school, with one event after another.*

Crowded means filled with people. *We were shoulder-to-shoulder in the crowded elevator.*

Packed can mean filled tightly. *The championship finals were played at a packed stadium.*

Stuffed can mean filled so tightly that it is hard to get things out. *The mailbox was stuffed with bills and junk mail.*

Jammed can mean filled more tightly than should be. *Spectators in the jammed courtroom gasped loudly at the man's confession.*

Crammed can mean jammed. *I tried to force one more tape into the video store's crammed drop box.*

ANTONYM: empty

WORDS AT PLAY

A baby sardine
Saw her first submarine.
She was scared as she watched
  through a peephole.

"Oh, come, come, come,"
Said the sardine's mum
"It's only a tin full of people."

—Spike Milligan

Funny

adjective

Funny means causing people to laugh or to be amused. *Tammy's funny story caused laughter all over the room.*

Amusing means mildly funny. *Aunt Tasha always starts her letters with amusing stories.*

Witty means funny in a clever way. *Shonelle's teacher often makes witty comments that the students enjoy.*

Laughable means causing people to laugh. It often suggests laughter that makes fun of someone. *Some people made serious posters for the contest, but a few made laughable sketches.*

Humorous means meant to be funny. *Richie likes humorous comic books better than adventure comics.*

Comical means funny in a happy way. *The circus clowns wear silly clothes and look very comical.*

Hilarious means very funny. *The hilarious movie made everyone laugh out loud.*

Ridiculous means so foolish that it is funny. *"Keep a cow in your bedroom? Don't be ridiculous,"* said Grandma.

SEE **laugh** for words for what you might do when something is funny.
ANTONYM: serious

A word bank is a list of words that share an idea. Suppose you want to write about circus clowns. You can start by making a word bank of all the words you think of when you think of clowns. Here are some words we thought of:

hilarious	ridiculous	comical	funny
silly	laughter	tricks	costume
grin	wig	shoes	gloves

When you plan what to write, your word bank will help you find ideas. When you are writing, your word bank will give you words, so you don't have to stop and think of them. This book can help you find words for the bank.

The circus clowns wear silly clothes and look very **comical.**

Get
verb

Get means to have something that you did not have before. *Mariana got some presents on her birthday. André got a hammer from the toolbox.*

Obtain means to get something by an effort. *Zena obtained the book from the library.*

Acquire means to get and own, usually by continued effort. *Ted acquired the baseball cards he wanted at a card trading show.*

Receive means to get something that has been given or sent or handed to you. *Sharon has received six letters from her pen pal.*

Fetch means to go and get something. *"Can Rover fetch a stick as big as that?" asked Lucy.*

Win can mean to get something by effort, skill, or luck. *My mother's team won first prize in the bowling league.*

Earn means to get something by working for it. *Stacy babysits to earn money. Mike earned a merit badge as a Boy Scout by cleaning up a park.*

Gain means to get something that is worth having. *Delbert gained many friends during his first year in the chess club.*

SEE **catch** for words that mean to grab hold of something.

Get is used in phrases that have special meanings:

Get along can mean to succeed, especially in liking each other. *Dyan and her new teacher get along very well.*

Get in can mean to arrive. *The plane got in an hour late.*

Get off can mean to avoid punishment. *The first time, you get off with just a warning.*

Get out of can mean to leave. *The sheriff gave the outlaws an hour to get out of town.* **Get out of** also can mean to learn from. *"What did you get out of the story, Leah?" asked Mrs. Dunstan.*

Get over means to feel better after something. *We will go on a trip when Paulie gets over the measles.*

Get up means to arise from bed. *It's still dark out when we get up for school in the winter.*

The sheriff gave the outlaws an hour to **get out of** town.

Go
verb

Go means to move from one place to another. *Ray goes to dancing class on Wednesdays.*

Go is also used in phrases that have special meanings. Each of these phrases has its own set of synonyms.

go after

The ducklings **follow** their mother everywhere.

Go after means to move toward someone or something. *When the ball is hit, our dog goes after it and brings it back.*

Follow can mean to move in the same direction as someone or something. *The ducklings follow their mother everywhere.*

Tail means to follow closely and secretly. *The detectives tailed the criminal to her hideout.*

Track and **trail** mean to follow, by marks or sound or smell. *Scientists are tracking two wolves to learn how far they move each day. The wolves sometimes trail a deer for hours.*

Chase means to follow fast and try to catch. *Mom chased our dog and got him back in the house.*

Pursue means to chase. It is a formal word. *The king pursued the white deer into the Forest of Shadows.*

go along

Go along means to move together with someone. *Rashid wants to go along when we visit the aquarium.*

Accompany means to go along with. *Dad and Mr. Monroe will accompany our team to the playoffs.*

Escort means to go along with. It is a formal word. *Secret Service agents escort the President everywhere.*

Attend can mean to go along with in order to serve. *Joan plays the part of the lady who attends the princess.*

Conduct can mean to go along with in order to lead the way. *An usher will conduct you to your seat.*

The wild horses **roam** across the land; they **rove** miles every day.

go around

WORD POOL

Here are some words for unusual ways to go. They are not synonyms, but they are related words. Use your dictionary to find their meanings.

crawl
creep
dance
glide
slide
slither
waddle
wade
wiggle
wriggle

Go around means to move from place to place. *Tad goes around at night to make sure the lights are off.*

Wander means to move here and there without purpose. *That woman has no place to live, so she wanders the streets.*

Stray means to leave the correct path or to move without purpose. *You must not stray in the woods, or you can get lost.*

Roam and **rove** mean almost the same as wander, but they often suggest long distances. *The wild horses roam across the land; they rove miles every day.*

Ramble means almost the same as wander. It suggests a happy, peaceful time. *Myung loves to ramble on the beach after school.*

SEE **leave** for words that mean to go away.

P.S.

Some of these phrases have other meanings, too:

Go along can mean to cooperate. *I don't really like their plans for the afternoon, but I'll go along with them.*

Go around can mean to be enough for everyone. *"Are there enough apples to go around, or shall I get some more?" asked Hetty.*

Shamira thinks the movie was **excellent** and hopes her friends will like it as much as she did.

Good
adjective

Good means well done or of high quality. *Joey worked very hard and made a good painting. Vicki is a very good softball player, so I hope she'll be on my team.*

Fine means very good. *Juan was happy when his teacher told him he had done a fine job.*

Excellent means extremely good. *Shamira thinks the movie was excellent and hopes her friends will like it as much as she did.*

Admirable means very good. *Scout Troop 97 did an admirable job of clearing trash from the park.*

SEE **fair** for words that mean honest to everyone.
SEE **great** for words that mean better than good.
SEE **nice** for words that mean pleasant.
ANTONYM: bad

The word *good* is often overused. See what happens in the paragraphs below when we replace *good* with more precise words. Some of the words that we have used come from the studies for **fair** and **great,** which the study for **good** tells you to see.

An Excellent
A ~~Good~~ Movie

First the good news. "The Girl Who Could Fly" is

fine
a ~~good~~ movie. The way it makes you believe in a 14-year-

admirable
old helicopter pilot is really ~~good.~~ Kathee Harris gives a

terrific
~~good~~ performance, especially in the funny parts.

fair
This wouldn't be a ~~good~~ review if it left out the bad

An unbiased
news. The movie has too many mushy love scenes. A ~~good~~

critic has to say that the movie would be a lot better

without them. Even so, go see this ~~good~~ movie for a good

time.

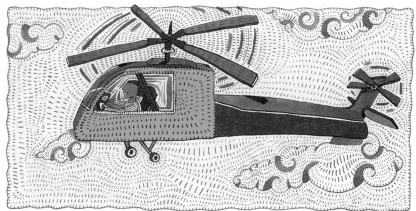

Great

adjective

Great means important, worthy of praise, or unusually good. *Braille was a great invention because it lets people read who cannot see. Most people agree that the Fourth of July is a great holiday.*

Wonderful can mean very, very good. *Lisa had a wonderful time at the party.*

Terrific can mean wonderful. It is a little less formal. *Cal wants more books by the writer of this terrific story.*

Tremendous can mean extremely pleasant and satisfying. *Coretta and Sonny say the fireworks were tremendous.*

Grand can mean of great quality. *Mrs. Patel always ends music class by playing some grand piece.*

SEE **big** for words that mean large.
SEE **good** for words that mean fine but not great.
SEE **huge** for words that mean bigger than big.
ANTONYMS: awful, dreadful, terrible

WORDS AT PLAY
• • • • • • • • • • • • • • • •
A little elephant went out one day
Upon a spider's web to play.
He had such tremendous fun,
He called for another elephant to come.

The word *great* is often overused. See what happens in the paragraph below when we replace *great* with more precise words. Some of the words that we have used come from the studies for **big, good,** and **huge,** which the study for **great** tells you to see.

Wonderful
A ~~Great~~ Trip

Mr. Silber's fifth-grade class had a ~~great~~ *wonderful* field trip to the art museum last week. The museum is a ~~great~~ *huge* ~~big~~ building, and it is full of ~~great~~ *large* pictures and statues. One painting, "A Table of Fruit," is especially ~~great~~ *fine*. The artist has painted it with ~~great~~ *admirable* skill, so everything you see

looks just like the real thing. All the kids in the class said it made them hungry. So we knew it was great art.

Group

noun

Group means a number of people, animals, or things gathered together. *A small group of birds chirped away in a tree.*

Bundle means a group of items tied or wrapped up. *A cleanup of the backyard produced several bundles of sticks and twigs.*

Bunch means a group of things of one kind, held or growing together. *I wish cherries grew in handy bunches like grapes.*

Cluster means items of one kind forming a small, tight group. *A little house stands amid a cluster of trees.*

Set means a group of things that belong together. *Ravi's birthday gift was a set of miniature railroad cars.*

herd

pride

school

pack

herd

WORD POOL

Here are some special words
for groups of animals.

a **brood** of chicks
a **covey** of quail
a **flock** of sheep
a **gaggle** of geese
a **herd** of cows or deer
a **litter** of kittens or puppies
a **pack** of wolves
a **pod** of seals or whales
a **pride** of lions
a **school** of dolphins or fish
a **swarm** of bees

school

pod

litter

flock

covey

group 95

Happy
adjective

Happy means feeling good and being pleased. *Juanita was happy to have made the junior softball team.*

Cheerful means happy and in good spirits. *Frank is still as cheerful as ever, even though he faces a serious operation.*

Glad means feeling pleasure because of something good. *Kendra was glad to be invited to the party.*

Delighted means very pleased with something. *Harry is delighted that his family is going to spend a weekend at the seashore.*

Merry means laughing and full of fun. *"We wish you a merry Christmas," sang the carolers.*

Jolly means cheerful and friendly. *Mrs. Timmins is my favorite teacher because she is always so jolly.*

ANTONYMS: sad, unhappy

"We wish you a **merry** Christmas," sang the carolers.

Hard
adjective

Hard means needing a lot of work or effort. *Cleaning out a garage is a hard job.*

Difficult means not easy to do or figure out. *The arithmetic problem was very difficult.*

Tough can mean very hard. *It was tough to carry all our stuff up two flights to the new apartment—but the extra bedroom makes it worthwhile.*

Backbreaking means extremely hard. *Getting all the garbage downstairs is a backbreaking job for the janitor.*

Rough can mean hard. *"Boy, that was one rough exam!" sighed Winnie.*

Strenuous can mean requiring great effort. *Going through the rapids is the most strenuous part of the river trip.*

ANTONYMS: easy, simple

Going through the rapids is the most **strenuous** part of the river trip.

Harm

verb

Harm means to cause pain or injury to someone or something. *Mother birds protect their nests from being harmed. Pollution harms the environment.*

Hurt means to wound someone or something. *Larry hurt the other team's player when they ran into each other.*

Injure means to hurt. *Gilda injured her knee when she tripped on the stairs.*

Damage means to harm something in a way that lessens its value. *Mike's bicycle was badly damaged when a delivery truck backed into it.*

SEE **break** for words that mean to come apart or knock apart.
SEE **destroy** for words that mean to break something to bits.
ANTONYM: help

Mike's bicycle was badly **damaged** when a delivery truck backed into it.

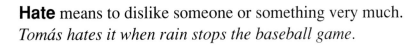

Hate

verb

Hate means to dislike someone or something very much. *Tomás hates it when rain stops the baseball game.*

Detest means to dislike someone or something strongly. *Petra detests bullies because they are cruel.*

Despise means to look down on and scorn a person or thing. *Paul despises people who cheat on exams.*

Abhor means to feel disgust and hatred for. *Jacob abhors cockroaches.*

ANTONYM: love

Tomás **hates** it when rain stops the baseball game.

Help

verb

Help means to do part of the work that someone else has to do. *"Can you help me with my homework this weekend?" asked Maud. Everyone helped get ready for the surprise party.*

Assist means to help someone do something by working with him or her. *Teachers' aides often assist teachers in the classroom.*

Aid means to give help that is needed. *Young people can often aid people who are sick.*

Lend a hand is an idiom that means to help someone do something. It is an informal phrase. *Phyllis lent her friend a hand with washing and drying the dishes.*

Everyone **helped** get ready for the surprise party.

Hide
verb

Hide means to put out of sight. *There were so many presents that it took half an hour to hide them all.*

Conceal means to hide something on purpose so that it won't be found. *Paul concealed his father's birthday present at the back of the closet.*

Bury can mean to hide something by putting it in a hole in the ground and then filling the hole. *My dog buries every bone she can find.*

Cover up can mean to keep something bad from being known. *The people who were selling the car tried to cover up its problems.*

ANTONYM: show

There were so many presents that it took half an hour to **hide** them all.

Nilda's collection **includes** stamps from many countries.

Hold
verb

Hold means to keep something inside. *"Will this cup hold as much as that glass?" inquired Mrs. Hobbes.*

Contain means to have something inside. *Dad's Irish stew contains lamb, potatoes, carrots, onions, and a lot more.*

Include means to have as a part or parts. *Nilda's collection includes stamps from many countries.*

Keep in means to hold and not let out. *"Will the dam keep in the flood waters?" asked the reporter.*

P.S.
• •

Hold is used in phrases that have special meanings:

Hold down means to keep something under control. *"Could you hold down that music while I'm on the telephone?" cried Barbara Ann.*

Hold out means to last or to continue. *We have enough hot dogs, but the buns won't hold out to the end of the night.*

Hold over means to make something happen longer than the expected time. *The store is holding over the sale until all the bathing suits are gone.*

Hold up can mean to cause delay. *This heavy traffic will probably hold up our bus.* **Hold up** can also mean to rob someone. *The police have caught the gang who held up the gas station.*

Hot
adjective

Hot means having or giving off much heat. *Tammy likes the water in her bath to be really hot.*

Burning means on fire or very hot. *The walls and roof of the burning house fell in with a roar. Dad says my forehead is burning, and I must have a fever.*

Fiery means hot as fire or on fire. *Police kept people away from the fiery crash on the highway.*

Blazing means burning brightly. *A fire is blazing in the fireplace.*

Scorching can mean extremely hot. *Rudy wears a straw hat to protect him from the scorching sun.*

ANTONYMS: cold, cool

P.S.

People sometimes use "hot" words to show that a feeling is very strong. Often that feeling is anger, but not always:

Her hot temper gets her into trouble.
Darryl has a burning desire to be a famous artist.
Ana María made a fiery speech demanding freedom for her country.
The two men had a blazing argument.
Bruce's report on pollution was filled with scorching rage.

Rudy wears a straw hat to protect him from the **scorching** sun.

Huge
adjective

Huge means very big. *The great white shark has huge jaws.*

Enormous means much larger than normal. *The enormous gorilla was one of the greatest attractions at the zoo.*

Monster can mean huge. It is an informal word. *The whole block of warehouses went up in a monster fire.*

Vast means covering a very wide area. *The Sahara is a vast desert in northern Africa.*

Immense means so big that it is hard to measure. *The Pacific Ocean is immense.*

Gigantic means greatly larger than other things of the same kind. *The gigantic shopping mall has space for over five hundred stores.*

SEE **big** for words that mean large, but smaller than huge.
ANTONYM: tiny

WORD STORY

Vast comes from a Latin word meaning "empty." A vast space often seems empty because it is so big.

WRITER'S CHOICE

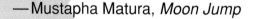

One night Cayal began to jump higher, and higher, and higher, until . . . with one enormous leap he jumped all the way to the moon.

—Mustapha Matura, *Moon Jump*

Why *enormous?* It would take a very big leap to get to the moon. Mustapha Matura uses *enormous* to show that Cayal's final leap is much bigger than his earlier ones.

Hurry
verb

Hurry means to move faster. *"Hurry or you'll be late for school, Cathy," said her mother.*

Rush means to move with speed or force. *Chelsea rushed out of school and wheeled herself quickly home to play with the new puppy.*

Hasten means to move quickly to do something. *Sandra hastened to answer the telephone.*

Speed means to go very fast. *The fire engines went speeding toward the blaze.*

WORD STORY

Hustle comes from a Dutch word meaning "to shake." When you hustle, you "shake a leg."

Hustle means to move quickly and with energy. *"If you want to go to the movie tonight, you'd better hustle with your chores, Jay," said his father.*

Shake a leg and **get a move on** are idioms that mean to hurry. They are informal phrases. *"Shake a leg, Mike; your friends are all waiting for you to get a move on," called his mother.*

SEE **eager** for words for why you might hurry.
SEE **quick** for words you might use about someone who is in a hurry.
SEE the Word Pool at **run** for words that mean to hurry on foot.
ANTONYMS: dawdle, slow down

Chelsea **rushed** out of school and wheeled herself quickly home to play with the new puppy.

By the river stood a busy village of many **huts.**

Hut
noun

Hut means a small house. Huts usually have only one or two rooms. They are made from natural materials. *By the river stood a busy village of many huts.*

Cabin means a hut. Cabins are usually built of wood. *Abraham Lincoln was born in a log cabin.*

Shed means a small building for keeping things in. A shed is usually smaller than a hut. *Anna put the bats and balls in the shed behind the gym.*

Shack means a hut or a shed. Shacks are built in a poor way out of poor materials. *A homeless man lives in that shack under the bridge.*

Idea
noun

Idea means a picture or plan in your mind. *I have an idea about what to do after school.*

Notion means an idea. It is often used for an idea that is not fully formed. *Jim had a notion that a class picnic might be fun.*

Thought means an idea about something. *Winona offered some thoughts on where to hold the picnic.*

Brainstorm means a sudden, very good idea. *Lisa just had a brainstorm—a picnic at the amusement park!*

Concept means a general idea of something. *"What is your concept of democracy, Moira?" asked Mrs. Jackson.*

Impression can mean an idea that is not very clear. *As we looked at the old house, we had the impression that we had seen it before.*

SEE **opinion** for words that mean someone's way of thinking.
SEE **think** for words that mean to have ideas.

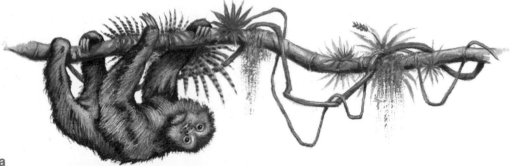

Interested

adjective

I was **fascinated** by the sweetpotato weevil in our science teacher's collection.

Interested means paying attention because you want to. *Patty's report kept the whole class interested.*

Attentive means paying attention. *Shonda learns quickly because she is so attentive.*

Absorbed means very interested. *Hector was absorbed all afternoon in his space adventure story.*

Fascinated means so interested by something that it is hard to turn your attention away from it. *I was fascinated by the sweetpotato weevil in our science teacher's collection.*

Spellbound means completely fascinated. *His grandmother's stories keep Jimmy spellbound.*

Engrossed means so interested that your entire attention is taken. *Carlo was so engrossed in the new video game that he didn't hear the doorbell ring.*

All eyes and ears is an idiom that means paying complete attention. *The students were all eyes and ears as they walked through the pretzel factory.*

ANTONYM: bored

WRITING TIP: Using Details

A word people use a lot is *interesting*. It's interesting to notice that sentences full of this word aren't usually very interesting to read.

> *We had an interesting trip to an interesting museum where we saw lots of interesting things.*

If you want people to know that something is interesting, the best way is to give details. Then your reader knows why you were interested.

> *At the museum we saw arrowheads, dinosaur eggs, and an Egyptian mummy. On the way back, we got lost. Then, the bus broke down.*

Job
noun

Job means work to do. *Claudine will be lucky to find a summer job that pays well.*

Task means a certain amount of assigned work to be done. *Mark's task was to unwind the string as the kite rose.*

Chore means a regular task. *Roger's chores include setting the table and taking out the garbage.*

Assignment means a certain amount of required work, especially schoolwork. *In science class, we have a written homework assignment every day.*

Errand means a job that includes making a trip. *Now that Dr. Muñoz works late at the hospital, her family buys groceries and does the other errands.*

SEE **work** for words that mean effort.

Mark's **task** was to unwind the string as the kite rose.

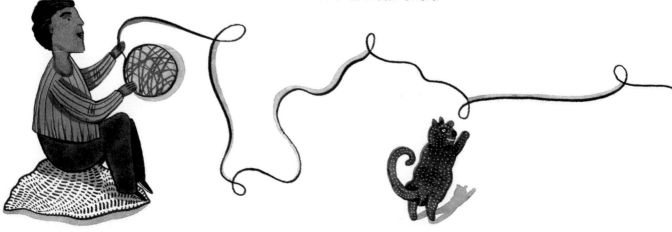

Join
verb

Jerilyn **attached** a long
tail to the kite.

Join means to put or bring things together. *The two wagon trains joined to cross the prairie together. Everyone in the game joined hands and formed a circle.*

Connect means to join things together, often so they touch at one place. *"Inez, please connect the keyboard to the computer," directed Ms. Panapoulis.*

Fasten means to make things stay touching each other. *"Wanda, fasten your mittens to your sleeves, please," said her mother.*

Attach means to fasten. *Jerilyn attached a long tail to the kite.*

Link means to connect as if by the loops of a chain. *When the caboose was linked up to the last freight car, the train pulled out.*

Combine means to put things or people together for a special purpose. *The combined efforts of 60 people made the carnival a success.*

Unite means to join into a single thing. *Thirteen colonies united to form one country.*

SEE **mix** for words that mean to make something out of other things.
ANTONYM: separate

I asked my mother
for fifteen cents,
To see the elephant
jump the fence.
He jumped so high,
He touched the sky,
And didn't come back
till the Fourth of July.

Jump
verb

Jump means to move suddenly through the air. *Charmaine jumped over the puddle.*

Leap means to jump high into the air. *My dog always leaps into my arms when I whistle.*

Spring means to jump quickly and gracefully. *The cat stole a sardine and sprang from the table to the floor.*

Bound means to move quickly with many jumps. *The deer bounded across the meadow and into the woods.*

Skip means to move quickly with one jump after another. *Darlene and Cho held hands and skipped down the street.*

Hop means to jump on one foot, or on both feet together. *A robin hopped along the window ledge and looked in our kitchen.*

Vault means to jump over something by using your hands or a pole. *Carol likes to vault the fence by grabbing it with her hands and swinging herself over.*

Hurdle means to jump over something while running. *In this race, the runners hurdle several low hedges.*

Keep

verb

Keep means to have and not get rid of something. *My sister keeps shoes long after they wear out.*

Withhold means to keep back and refuse to give. It is a formal word. *I shall withhold part of your allowance to pay for the broken window.*

Hold can mean to keep in and not let out. *Gino can hold his breath and swim across the pool underwater.*

Save can mean to keep and put away. *I am saving money for a new game cartridge.*

Hang on to means to refuse to get rid of something. *Junko hangs on to every comic book she gets.*

Hold on to means to hang on to. *Billie held on to her baseball glove until it was too small for her.*

Know

verb

WORDS FROM WORDS

acknowledge
acknowledgment
know
knowable
know-how
knowing
knowingly
know-it-all
knowledge
know-nothing
unknowable
unknowingly

Know means to have facts about something or someone. *My sister knows how to speak two languages. I know that our new neighbor just moved here from the Philippines.*

Understand can mean to know something well. *Richard understands sign language and likes to see it used in plays.*

Realize means to know that something is true. *Leaping Water realized that she had wandered far from the village.*

Recognize can mean to realize. *I recognize that I hurt Karen's feelings, and I'm sorry.*

Richard **understands** sign language and likes to see it used in plays.

Last
adjective

Last means after all others, or coming at the end. *Mandy ate the last apple, leaving the bowl empty. The last month of the year is December.*

Final means last. It emphasizes that there are no more to come. *Del scored the winning points in the final second of the game.*

Latest can mean most recent or last up to this time. *"Have you seen the latest music video by that awesome singer?" asked Marika.*

Closing can mean last. *The closing scene of the movie scared Mookie, who was glad when it ended.*

Concluding means last. *In the concluding chapter, the author reveals how the murder was committed—and by whom!*

Ultimate means last, especially as part of a process. *Toni is learning to play the piano because her ultimate goal is to write songs.*

SEE **end** for words that mean to reach the last part.
SEE **stop** for words that mean to make something end.
ANTONYM: first

Del scored the winning points in the **final** second of the game.

Laugh
verb

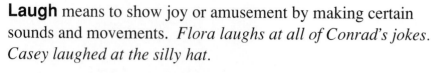

Laugh means to show joy or amusement by making certain sounds and movements. *Flora laughs at all of Conrad's jokes. Casey laughed at the silly hat.*

Chuckle means to laugh very quietly or softly. *Lukas and Julie chuckled as they finished reading the comic strip.*

Giggle means to laugh in a silly way, with short, high-pitched sounds. *All the kindergarten children giggled when they saw the funny puppet show.*

Snicker means to laugh but try to cover it up, or laugh in a sly way. *The villain in the TV show snickered when the hero was trapped.*

Roar can mean to laugh loudly, in uncontrolled amusement. *The circus crowd roared as more and more clowns tumbled out of the tiny car.*

Crack up is an idiom that can mean to laugh long and hard. *This new TV show is so funny, it will make you crack up.*

SEE **funny** for words for why you might laugh.

WRITING TIP: Words That Imitate Sounds

One way to liven up your writing is to use words that imitate sounds. For example, if you were writing about someone laughing, you might use words such as *chuckle, giggle, snicker,* and *guffaw.* If you were writing about night sounds at the pond in the park, you might use imitative words such as *plop, splash,* and *rustle.*

Leave
verb

Leave means to go away from where you are. *A commuter train to Chicago leaves from this station every hour.*

Depart means to leave. It is a formal word. *The President departs for Washington today.*

Withdraw means to leave, often because you have to. *Under heavy attack from the enemy, the soldiers withdrew.*

Desert means to leave when it is wrong to leave. *Just when our band got a job, the drummer deserted us.*

Abandon can mean to leave suddenly. It suggests going away from a problem with no idea of returning. *Andy abandoned the jigsaw puzzle when the rain stopped.*

WORD STORY

Vamoose comes from "vamos," a Spanish word meaning "let's go." People who did not speak Spanish thought that they heard "vamoose."

Vamoose means to leave very quickly and suddenly. It is slang. *When Jim started doing cannonballs, the fish vamoosed.*

Run out on is an idiom that means to leave someone suddenly, usually just when they need you. *The sheriff chose deputies who would not run out on him.*

SEE **go** for words that mean to move from place to place.
ANTONYM: arrive

When Jim started doing cannonballs, the fish **vamoosed.**

Let
verb

Let means to allow or to permit. *If our homework is done, Dad will let us go to the movies.*

Let is also used in phrases that have special meanings. Each of these phrases has its own set of synonyms.

let down

Let down means to hurt the feelings of someone who trusts you. *She promised to help me with my science project, and she didn't let me down.*

Disappoint can mean not to keep a promise to someone. *Jojo promised to help with the posters; I hope he doesn't disappoint us!*

Fail can mean to be of no use when needed. *We had to use the clothesline when our dryer failed.*

Betray can mean to hurt someone who trusts you, on purpose. *"I'll tell you my secret if you promise not to betray me,"* whispered Bennett.

We had to use the clothesline when our dryer **failed.**

let off

Let off means to allow someone to avoid punishment or responsibility. *Davey was supposed to help with the shopping, but his father let him off so he could go to the carnival.*

Excuse can mean to let off. *On the day of her piano lesson, Rosita is excused from helping out with dinner.*

Pardon means to set free from punishment. *The governor pardoned the prisoner.*

let on

Let on means to allow something to be known. *"Don't let on to LaToya that we're planning a party for her," said Nick.*

Reveal means to make something known. *Maria revealed to Sally that she wants to be her best friend.*

Admit means to say that something is true, especially something that you feel bad about. *I admitted to my mother that I forgot the shopping list.*

Confess can mean to say that you have done wrong. *"Whoever took my book better confess now," said Judy.*

let out

The moth **freed** itself from the cocoon and hung there until its wings dried.

Let out means to allow someone to leave someplace. *Class will be let out early today so that everyone can help with school cleanup.*

Release can mean to let out. *When Andy got stuck in the railing, the janitor came to release him.*

Dismiss means to tell someone to leave. *Ms. Tran said she would dismiss us as soon as we were quiet.*

Free means to release someone or something that has been tightly held. *The moth freed itself from the cocoon and hung there until its wings dried.*

let up

Let up means to become less or to grow slower. *Steve's headache began to let up after an hour or so.*

Lessen means to make or become less. *My hopes of winning the spelling bee lessened when they asked me to spell "allegiance."*

Decrease means to lessen. *The price of summer clothes decreases in September.*

Diminish means to make or become smaller. *As the airplane went up, the buildings seemed to diminish beneath us.*

Andrea **likes** the dollhouse she got as a birthday present.

Like
verb

Like means to be pleased with someone or something. *Andrea likes the dollhouse she got as a birthday present.*

Enjoy means to take pleasure in something. *Katherine can enjoy swimming and diving with her new artificial leg.*

Fancy means to like something and to want it or choose it. *Howard fancies the idea of going to a baseball game and then a movie.*

Be fond of means to like something or someone very much. *I've always been fond of sherbet.*

SEE **love** for words that mean the feeling you have when you like someone or something very much.

ANTONYM: dislike

In the dollhouse Ruth saw a **little** chair like the big chairs in her own house.

Little

adjective

Little means not big, or less than normal in size. *In the dollhouse Ruth saw a little chair like the big chairs in her own house.*

Small means little. *Connie's small glass holds only five ounces of water. Some people consider Cornelius small for his age.*

Wee means very little. It is used mostly in stories, songs, and poems. *The wee people included the elves in the garden.*

Short can mean not tall. *Kenny is not too short to reach that high shelf.*

Skimpy means too little to be enough. *The skimpy snack left Amanda hungry.*

SEE **tiny** for words that mean even smaller than little.
ANTONYMS: big, large

Live
verb

Live means to have a home in a certain place. *Sheila lives on Maple Street.*

Dwell is a formal word that means to live. *Some desert people dwell in tents.*

Reside is also a formal word. It means to live in one place over a period of time. *The President resides in the White House while in office.*

Stay can mean to live somewhere for a while as a guest. *Ms. Pappas stays in hotels when she travels on business.*

Lodge means to live in a place for a short time. *My sister lodged with a French family on her trip to Paris.*

house

townhouses

igloo

pueblo

farmhouse

apartment building

WORD POOL

People live in many different kinds of homes. Here are some of them:

apartment building
cabin
cottage
farmhouse
hacienda
hogan
house
housing project
hut
igloo
kraal
mobile home
palace
pueblo
ranch house
shack
tepee
townhouse
villa
yurt

Look

verb

Look means to take in by eye. *"Look at the size of the fish I just caught!" exclaimed Dana.*

Watch means to look at carefully for a period of time. *Reba watched the jugglers perform with hoops and balls.*

Glance means to look quickly. *I glanced in Juan's direction, but he didn't notice me.*

View means to watch for a reason. *The robbery victim viewed a lineup of five suspects.*

Gaze means to watch steadily. It is used to show a strong attraction to what is watched. *The baby gazed in wonder at the butterfly.*

Stare means to watch steadily and directly, usually without blinking. *The children stared at the dinosaur skeleton in the natural history museum.*

SEE **see** for words that mean to know with your eyes.

WRITER'S CHOICE

Then he walked over to the candy jars for a closer look. There he stood staring at them with a hungry longing even though he knew good and well there would be no candy for him this day.

—Mildred D. Taylor, *The Friendship*

Why *staring?* Candy is a most unusual sight for this poor country boy. Mildred Taylor uses *staring* to show that he can't take his eyes off the jars full of sweets.

Here are some more words for ways you might look at something or someone. They are not synonyms, but are related words. Use your dictionary to find their meanings.

gape	glower	peek
gawk	goggle	peer
glare	ogle	squint

Loud
adjective

Loud means having or making a big sound. *Barbara doesn't like loud music.*

Noisy means with a lot of loud, harsh sounds. *The noisy traffic bothered June's father.*

Deafening means loud enough to hurt the ears. *Inga plugged her ears to block out the deafening sound of the fireworks.*

Thunderous can mean with a loud noise that sounds like thunder. *We heard the thunderous waterfall before we saw it.*

SEE **noise** for words that mean a loud sound.
SEE **shout** for words that mean to use a loud voice.
ANTONYM: quiet

▼
WRITING TIP: Descriptive Writing
• •

When you describe a person, a place, or a thing, you want your readers to imagine clearly what you are describing. Choosing lively, exact words can help. Suppose you are describing a baseball game:

The crowd gave a loud cheer when the star came to bat, and a very loud roar when he hit a home run.

Synonyms for the general word *loud* make the description stronger:

The crowd gave a thunderous cheer when the star came to bat, and a deafening roar when he hit a home run.

Inga plugged her ears to block out the **deafening** sound of the fireworks.

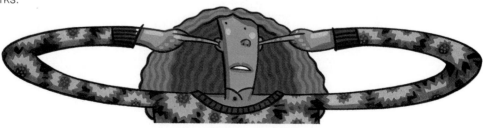

This picture of my family shows the **love** we feel for each other.

Love
noun

Love means a strong and tender feeling of liking or being fond of someone. *This picture of my family shows the love we feel for each other.*

Affection means a kind, warm feeling for someone or something. It is not as strong a word as love. *LuAnn shows affection for her dog by playing with him and caring for him.*

Fondness means liking or affection. *Ricardo and his grandparents share a fondness for ranchero music.*

Devotion means a very loyal feeling of love, either for someone or for something. *Angie's devotion to gymnastics leaves her little time for other sports.*

SEE **like** for words that mean to have a fondness for.
ANTONYMS: hate, hatred

Mad
adjective

Mad means feeling anger. *Jamie's father gets mad if she forgets to do her chores.*

Angry means the same as mad. *Nancy will be angry if Jan tells her secret.*

Sore can mean mad. *Lawan is sore because she fell down and got her new skirt dirty.*

Irritated means bothered or made somewhat angry. *Wayne became irritated when he had to wait a long time in the cafeteria line.*

Furious means wildly angry. *Getting stung by the bees made the grizzly bear furious.*

Exasperated means greatly annoyed or irritated. *Ushi became exasperated when her baby sister threw her cup on the floor for the fourth time.*

Fit to be tied is an idiom that means very angry. *When Mr. Barberio couldn't find his fishing rod, he was fit to be tied.*

SEE **anger** for words for what you feel when you're mad.
SEE **cross** for words that mean in a bad mood.

Main

adjective

WORDS FROM WORDS

main
mainframe
mainland
mainline
mainly
mainmast
mainsail
mainspring
mainstay
mainstream

Main means most important. *One main switch controls all the lights in this building.*

Major means more important than most others. *Major roads carry thousands of cars every hour.*

Chief means first in rank. *Who is the chief justice of the Supreme Court?*

Principal means first in order of importance. *The principal character in the movie "Home Alone" saves his family's house from burglars.*

Leading means most important and directing others. *The leading citizens of the town supported the mayor's plan.*

Top means highest or best. *Who is the top scorer on your bowling team?*

Major roads carry thousands of cars every hour.

Hal and Sandra **made** a fancy sand castle.

Make

verb

WORD STORY

Manufacture comes from two Latin words meaning "to make by hand." Today, *manufacture* usually means "to make by machine."

Make means to put something together or to give form to something. *Hal and Sandra made a fancy sand castle.*

Shape means to make something by giving it a form. *This machine takes clay and shapes it into bricks for another machine to bake.*

Build and **construct** mean to make something from materials and according to a plan. *Carpenters build houses, and engineers construct bridges.*

Manufacture means to create something from materials, over and over. *My mom works for a company that manufactures artificial arms and legs.*

Assemble can mean to make an object by fitting parts where they belong. *Roy and Ginnie assembled the model car by following the diagram.*

Form means to make, especially by hand. *Manuel formed a vase out of clay.*

Put together means to assemble. *Barbara put together the bookcase by herself.*

ANTONYMS: destroy, take apart

Many

adjective

Many means made up of a large number. *There were many apples on the tree before the harvest.*

Numerous means many. It emphasizes the large number. *At the library I saw numerous books about space travel, and I checked out two.*

Countless means so many that they can hardly be counted. *In the summer night, countless fireflies flew about, flickering their tiny lights.*

Quite a few means many. *Quite a few people were at the movie, but we still found seats.*

A lot of and **lots of** mean a great number or amount of. These are informal phrases. *There were a lot of fans at last night's ball game, and lots of them stayed for the fireworks.*

Oodles of means many. It is also an informal phrase. *When DeWayne bakes a cake, he puts oodles of raisins in it.*

ANTONYM: few

WORD POOL

Many words mean "many." Here are some more of them. These synonyms are all informal. Try using each one instead of "oodles" in the example sentence at that entry.

billions
heaps
jillions
loads
millions
scads
tons
trillions
umpteen
zillions

WORDS AT PLAY

Oodles of Noodles

I love noodles. Give me oodles.
Make a mound up to the sun.
Noodles are my favorite foodles.
I eat noodles by the ton.

—Lucia and James L. Hymes, Jr.

It was a **mistake** to leave the cake where the dog could get it.

Mistake

noun

Mistake means something you do wrong. *It was a mistake to leave the cake where the dog could get it.*

Error means a mistake. *Francesca made no errors on her geography test.*

Slip can mean a mistake, especially in speaking. *In a slip of the tongue, I called Dick, "Duck."*

Blunder means a careless or stupid mistake. *"Do you remember Mr. Hawker's blunder, when he locked us all out of the classroom?" Tom asked Josh.*

Booboo means a foolish mistake. It is slang. *Forgetting to put gas in the car was a real booboo.*

Luisa **blended** the flour and eggs and other ingredients to make a cake.

mix
verb

Mix means to put two or more things together. *There is always a bowl of mixed candies in Grandma's living room.*

Mingle means to mix, especially many things together. *The flavors of the meat, vegetables, and spices mingle in the stew.*

Blend means to mix thoroughly. *Luisa blended the flour and eggs and other ingredients to make a cake.*

Merge means to become completely mixed with something else. *The two toy manufacturers merged into one larger company.*

SEE **join** for words that mean to put together.
ANTONYM: separate

Move

verb

Move means to change the position of something. *Nicole moved her chair closer to the table.*

Shift means to move something to a different place or position, especially one nearby. *Annie shifted on the cushion, trying to get comfortable.*

Transfer means to change the position of something. *Chuck transferred his loose change from one pocket to the other.*

Remove means to move something from one place to another. *Luisa removed the cake carefully from the oven.*

SEE **pull** for words that mean to move something toward you.
SEE **push** for words that mean to move something away from you.
SEE **put** for words that mean to move something to a certain place.

Luisa **removed** the cake carefully from the oven.

Mystery

noun

WORD STORY

Mystery comes from a Greek word meaning "to close the lips or the eyes." That's a pretty good way to keep something a mystery.

Mystery means something that has not been explained or cannot be completely understood. *Where Brock was hiding was a mystery to the younger children. One of the great mysteries of science is why dinosaurs became extinct.*

Problem can mean a difficult question or a mystery. *The police have solved the problem of where the money was hidden.*

Puzzle means a baffling or challenging problem. *The zookeeper faced a puzzle—why the lion was so upset.*

Riddle means a trick question that requires clever thinking to answer. *The princess had to solve the wizard's riddle before she could enter the magic forest.*

Secret can mean a mystery or something hidden from your knowledge. *Jill wanted to find out the secret of how a chameleon changes color.*

The zookeeper faced a **puzzle**—why the lion was so upset.

Naughty
adjective

WORD STORY

Mischievous comes from an old French word meaning "to come to grief." Indeed, mischievous people sometimes do.

Naughty means not behaving well or not nice. *Ted was naughty, so he doesn't get cake.*

Bad can mean not behaving well. *When Wendy's dog chews on her shoes, she calls him a bad dog.*

Disobedient means not obeying or not willing to obey. *The disobedient girl did not do as she was told.*

Mischievous means taking pleasure from behaving badly. *The mischievous monkey kept pulling the lion's tail.*

Disorderly can mean making trouble. *When the team lost a close game, disorderly fans shouted at the referee.*

Rowdy means disorderly or quarrelsome. *If the people at the party get rowdy, the neighbors may call the police.*

SEE **wicked** for words that mean evil.
ANTONYMS: well-behaved, nice

The **mischievous** monkey kept pulling the lion's tail.

Neat

adjective

WORD STORY

Neat comes from a Latin word meaning "shining." Something that isn't neat usually isn't clean or shiny, either.

Neat means clean and in order. *After Winona put away her toys and clothes, the room was neat. Josie's baseball uniform always looks neat before a game.*

Orderly means neat. *If Bob kept his desk orderly, he could find things more easily.*

Tidy means neat and arranged in a pleasing way. *Grandma's room at the nursing home is tidy and bright.*

Trim means neat and in good condition. *Aunt Merry keeps her sailboat trim by making all repairs right away.*

Shipshape means trim. *Nicki and her classmates help Ms. Troy keep the classroom shipshape by cleaning up every single day.*

Uncluttered means neat and without many things around. *After our garage sale, the house looked uncluttered.*

Neat as a pin is an idiom that means very, very neat, with nothing out of place. *In a few minutes Grandpa made his workbench neat as a pin.*

ANTONYM: messy

WORDS AT PLAY

And They Met in the Middle

There was a young fellow named Pete
Who wasn't what I would call neat.
    One rumple worked down
    From the top of his crown,
And another worked up from his feet.

—John Ciardi

Jennifer loves the taste of **fresh** corn in the summer.

New

adjective

New means very recently made, become known, or come into existence. *A new movie starring the Fantastic Frogs has just been made. "Who is this new singer you like so much?" asked Mrs. Saghis. Tomorrow will be a new day.*

Brand-new means very new. *Ben hasn't even worn his brand-new sweater yet.*

Fresh means newly picked or made and not yet affected by time or use. *Jennifer loves the taste of fresh corn in the summer.*

Original can mean new or of a new kind. *Charles likes to make up original poems after he reads some famous old ones.*

WORD STORY

Modern comes from a Latin word meaning "just now."

Modern means of the present time or not far in the past. *Modern clothes are not like the clothes of one hundred years ago.*

Up-to-date means keeping up with new styles, ideas, or methods. *Shermika wants an up-to-date book about computers.*

ANTONYM: old

Nice

adjective

We had a **lovely** time at summer camp.

WORD STORY

Sympathetic comes from Greek words meaning "to feel together." This is what sympathetic people do.

Nice means pleasing or good. It is a very general word. *The salesclerk said, "Have a nice day." It was nice of Rich to remember Bonnie's birthday.*

Pleasant means giving pleasure and enjoyment. *Sue spent a pleasant afternoon with her friends. Gino always has a pleasant word for everyone.*

Enjoyable means giving a feeling of enjoyment and happiness. *This is a very enjoyable movie.*

Lovely can mean pleasing and delightful. *We had a lovely time at summer camp.*

Agreeable means pleasant and fun to be with. *Tom is a very agreeable person, and we like to visit him.*

Good-natured means having a kind and pleasant personality. *Mario is very good-natured and often helps his friends.*

Likable means pleasant and easy to like. *Shonna is a very likable girl, and I voted for her for class president.*

Friendly means pleasant and liking other people. *Barry is friendly to everyone in the class and is quite popular.*

Kind means friendly and full of sympathy. *He is a kind person and always tries to help people.*

Sympathetic means able to understand how other people feel. *Nina's sympathetic nature makes her an excellent nurse.*

Thoughtful can mean kind and considerate of others. *It was very thoughtful of John to hold the elevator door for the lady in the wheelchair.*

ANTONYMS: nasty, unpleasant

The word *nice* is often overused. See what happens in the paragraphs below when we replace *nice* with more precise words.

A ~~Nice~~ [Pleasant] Way to Spend Vacation

I had a really very ~~nice~~ [pleasant] summer vacation, because I went to a nice day camp. It was my first time, and everyone was ~~nice~~ [kind] to me.

My best friend there was Lisabet, who is a ~~nice~~ [likable] girl that everyone wants to be friends with. It was nice that she chose me to be her friend.

The counselors were all ~~nice~~ [friendly]. I liked Mr. Denton for the ~~nice~~ [sympathetic] way he listens when you have a problem.

I miss camp, but I guess it's nice to be back in school, too.

Noise

noun

WORD POOL

Here are some words for different kinds of quiet sounds. Use your dictionary to find out exactly what they mean. People often find quiet sounds pleasant to hear.

hum
mumble
murmur
patter
purr
rustle
sigh
swish
whisper

Noise means an unpleasant sound. *The noise of traffic woke Jason up.*

Racket means a clattering noise. *The carpenter hammering nails couldn't help making a racket.*

Uproar can mean the loud yelling of a crowd. *There was an uproar when the umpire called the runner out on a close play at third base.*

Rumpus means noisy disturbance. *"Mia, tell your brothers to stop that rumpus!" called Mr. Salafsky.*

SEE **loud** for words that mean with a big sound.
SEE **shout** for words that mean to use a loud voice.
ANTONYM: silence

WORD POOL

Here are some words for different kinds of loud sounds. Use your dictionary to find out exactly what they mean. Most people find loud sounds unpleasant to hear.

bang	**clash**
blare	**clatter**
blast	**crash**
boom	**din**
clamor	**jangle**
clang	**rattle**
clank	

The carpenter hammering nails couldn't help making a **racket**.

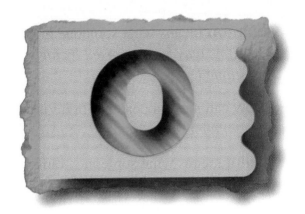

Old
adjective

Old means having lived for a long time. *The old woman can remember when cars and phones were very rare.*

Aged means having lived a very long time. *Ling's aged grandparents live with her and her parents.*

Elderly means old. *The elderly women have been friends for many years.*

Getting on in years is an idiom that means old. *Grandfather is getting on in years, so he exercises to stay strong and fit.*

SEE **ancient** for words that mean very old.
ANTONYM: young

The **elderly** women have been friends for many years.

Opinion
noun

Opinion means what someone thinks about something. *Opinions may be supported by facts, but they still can be questioned.*

View can mean a personal opinion. *Brad's view that sign language is easy is based on using it with his brother.*

Belief means what someone holds to be true. It is a stronger word than opinion. *Carrie shares her sister's belief that recycling is important.*

Judgment means an opinion based on considering and deciding. *In Martin's judgment, the soccer team needs to practice kicking goals.*

Attitude means the way that someone thinks and feels about something. *Concha has a positive attitude about going to a new school and expects to do well there.*

SEE **idea** for words that mean a thought.
SEE **think** for words that mean to have ideas and opinions.

Carrie shares her sister's **belief** that recycling is important.

Pain
noun

Pain means the bad feeling you have when you hurt yourself or when you are sick. *Michiko felt a lot of pain in her skinned knee after falling off her bicycle.*

Ache means a steady pain. *The ache in Arthur's tooth lasted until the dentist filled it.*

Soreness means pain. *Gargling with hot water and salt helped the soreness in Fiona's throat.*

WORD STORY

Twinge comes from an old English word meaning "to pinch." A twinge may feel as if someone suddenly pinched you.

Twinge means a sudden pain. *Gretchen felt a twinge in her ankle just after doing the long jump.*

Stitch can mean a sharp pain, usually along your side. *Alberto ran hard to win the race but then bent over with a stitch in his side.*

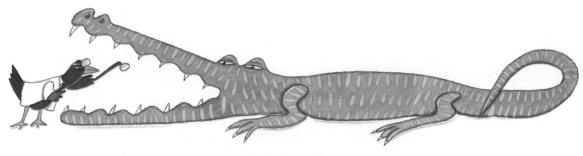

Arthur has an **ache** in his tooth.

The sheep are grazing in **part** of the field.

Part
noun

Part means some piece or amount that is less than the whole. *The sheep are grazing in part of the field.*

Portion means a part. *Scott and Hanako each got a portion of the prize money. "Cut the meat loaf so that there is a portion for everyone, Victoria," directed her grandmother.*

Section means a part, especially one that can be considered or handled by itself. *This section of Uncle Clint's garden looks like a Japanese garden.*

Segment means a section. It often suggests that something has parts naturally and in each case. *Each segment of a grapefruit has a thin skin.*

Fraction means an equal part of a whole. *We are learning to multiply fractions in class this year.*

Share means the part that belongs to each person. *Britney wants to do her fair share of the work.*

SEE **piece** for more words that mean a bit of something.
ANTONYM: whole

Perfect

adjective

WORDS FROM WORDS

imperfect
imperfection
imperfectly
perfect
perfectable
perfectly
perfection
perfectionism
perfectionist

Perfect means having no faults or being the best. *Today is a perfect day. Yael turned in a perfect paper.*

Flawless means not having any faults. *This new computer program is flawless.*

Faultless means flawless. *The gymnast's performance was faultless in every way.*

Foolproof means made so that nothing can go wrong. *Anyone can bake a cake with this foolproof recipe.*

Ideal means perfect. *This patch of woods is the ideal spot for our picnic.*

SEE **great** for words that mean almost as good as perfect.
ANTONYM: imperfect

The gymnast's performance was **faultless** in every way.

P.S.

Perfect is used in phrases that have special meanings:

A **perfect game** is a baseball game in which one team gets no batter on base.

Perfect pitch is the ability to recognize exactly any musical note you hear.

A **perfect number** is the sum of all numbers that go into it evenly, except itself. One, two, and three go into six. One plus two plus three equals six. To a mathematician, six is a "perfect" number.

The quilt was made from **scraps** of cloth that Grandma had saved.

Piece
noun

Piece means a small part of something larger, or one thing among others like it. *José picked up the pieces of the broken cup. A chess game begins with 32 pieces on the board.*

Fragment means a part that has been broken off. *Jimee once dug a fragment of an arrowhead out of the ground.*

Bit means a small piece of something larger. *Robin found two whole crackers and another one broken into bits.*

Crumb means a tiny piece of bread or cake, broken from a larger piece. *After dinner there were some crumbs on the table.*

Scrap means a little bit, especially of something that is left over. *The quilt was made from scraps of cloth that Grandma had saved.*

Lump means a small, solid piece of material. *Our snowman's eyes are lumps of coal.*

Chunk means a thick lump. *Misty threw a chunk of wood into the campfire.*

Chip means a thin small piece. *A chip of paint fell off the wall in Jay's room.*

SEE **part** for more words that mean a bit of something.

Plan
noun

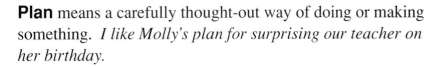

Plan means a carefully thought-out way of doing or making something. *I like Molly's plan for surprising our teacher on her birthday.*

Program can mean a plan going from one step or event to the next. *Our city's program for clearing up dump sites went smoothly.*

Undertaking means a plan of great imagination, danger, or difficulty. *Feeding our neighbor's six dogs was quite an undertaking for Missy.*

Enterprise means a bold undertaking. *This business enterprise will cost me lots of money if it fails.*

Scheme means a plan of carefully chosen details. *Uncle Joe has a scheme to save on groceries by growing his own vegetables.*

Plot means a secret plan, especially to do something evil. *Police uncovered a plot to rob the bank.*

SEE **idea** for words that mean what you need for a good plan.
SEE **think** for words that mean how you come up with a plan.

WORDS AT PLAY

If you plan to land a spaceship on the moon
I hope your enterprise succeeds quite soon.
But if you're hot on a plot
To run to the sun
I doubt that your scheme will be much fun.

Play

noun

Play means anything you do for enjoyment with your body or your mind. *Recess is time for play between classes.*

Fun means a good time or amusement. *We all had fun at the county fair.*

Game means anything played for fun. *Nicholas prefers a game of tag to hide-and-seek.*

Sport means any game or contest played for fun. A sport usually has set rules. *Sharon's favorite sport is hockey.*

Pastime means anything you do to enjoy yourself by passing time pleasantly. *Aunt Sarah's favorite pastime is knitting.*

Hobby means something that interests you a lot and that you do because you enjoy it. *Arturo's hobby is collecting baseball cards.*

ANTONYM: work

We all had **fun** at the county fair.

Roger is too **broke** to go to a movie.

Poor
adjective

Poor means having little or no money. *A poor person may not have a lot of clothes to wear.*

Penniless means without any money, even if only for a short time. *Isabel was penniless after spending the last cent of her allowance.*

Broke is an informal word that can mean without money. *Roger is too broke to go to a movie.*

Needy means poor and not having enough to live on. *The needy family receives food stamps from the government.*

Poverty-stricken means poor and not able to do anything about it. *Poverty-stricken after the crops failed, the family lost their farm.*

ANTONYMS: rich, wealthy

Promise
verb

WORD STORY

Agree comes from old French words meaning "to your liking." If a suggestion is to your liking, you'll probably agree to it.

Promise means to give your word to someone that you will or will not do something. *I promised to go to the zoo with Ted next Saturday.*

Agree can mean to promise to do something that someone else wants. *I agreed to play tennis with her.*

Pledge means to promise something in a sincere, solemn way. *Aunt Rita pledged twenty dollars to the animal shelter.*

Vow means to pledge. *Hester vowed never to forget Lucia's birthday again.*

Swear can mean to make a serious pledge or vow. The word often is used about a person who makes an official oath. *A person under oath swears to tell only the truth.*

I **promised** to go to the zoo with Ted next Saturday.

Pull
verb

Pull means to make something move toward you, or follow along behind you. *The tractor pulls a plow.*

Tug means to pull hard, sometimes stopping to rest between pulls. *Samira tugged at the door that was stuck.*

Jerk means to pull quickly and suddenly. *Al jerked his arm away from the cage when the tiger came close.*

Drag means to pull something along the ground or floor. *Ruth dragged a heavy chair across the room.*

Haul means to pull something big or heavy for a long distance. *A locomotive must be very powerful to haul that long line of boxcars.*

Tow means to pull something along behind a car or whatever you're riding in. *The Flores family towed a boat behind their car.*

SEE **move** for words that mean to change where something is.
ANTONYM: push

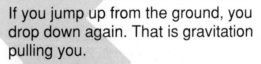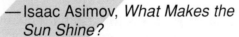

WRITER'S CHOICE

If you jump up from the ground, you drop down again. That is gravitation pulling you.

—Isaac Asimov, *What Makes the Sun Shine?*

Why *pulling?* Isaac Asimov uses *pulling* to show that things don't just fall toward the Earth. The Earth makes them fall. The other words have added meanings, but the meaning of *pull* is as basic as the law of gravity.

While Betty tugged on the reins, Buster tried to **push** the stubborn mule from behind.

Push

verb

Push means to move something away from you. *While Betty tugged on the reins, Buster tried to push the stubborn mule from behind.*

Nudge means push gently. *Tracey nudged Dee Ann with her elbow to get her attention.*

Shove means to push hard against something or someone. *Billy shoved the dirty clothes into his laundry bag.*

Thrust means to push hard and quickly. *The firefighters thrust open the doors of the burning house.*

Propel means to push foward with a steady force. *Rockets propel a spacecraft as it lifts off a launching pad.*

SEE **move** for words that mean to change where something is.
ANTONYM: pull

Put

verb

Put means to move something to some place. *"Marta, please put the flowers in this vase," asked Ms. Vanberg. Juan put his crutches on the floor next to his chair.*

Place means to put something in a certain spot. *Julie placed the heavy dish very carefully in the center of the table.*

Set means to put something in a certain position. *The furniture movers carefully set the piano next to the wall.*

Lay means to put something in a horizontal or lying-down position. *My brother and I helped my uncle lay the new carpet.*

Stick means to put something somewhere in a hurry. *"That's the fire drill bell, class, so stick your books under your desk and line up at the door," announced Mr. Dolan.*

SEE **move** for words that mean to change where something is.

Charles **put in** an hour straightening up his room.

P.S.

Put is used in phrases that have special meanings:

Put in can mean to spend an amount of time. *Charles put in an hour straightening up his room.*

Put off can mean to postpone something. *The PTA meeting has been put off until next week because of the snow.*

Put on can mean to make some public event happen. *Deon and Cheryl want to be in the play that the sixth graders will put on.*

Quick
adjective

Quick means moving, happening, or done in a short time. *With a quick turn, the driver avoided hitting the other car.*

Fast means moving with much speed. *Our track team has many fast runners, so our school wins most races.*

Rapid means very quick. It is used mostly to describe motion. *Sam walked at a rapid pace when he heard the bell.*

Speedy means very quick. It is often used for things that you want to happen or to be finished. *Martin was sick, but he made a speedy recovery.*

Swift means very fast. *She fielded the ball and threw to first base in one swift motion.*

Hasty means quick and with not enough time or thought. *His hasty decision caused problems later.*

SEE **hurry** for words that mean to go fast.
SEE **suddenly** for words that mean before you know it.
ANTONYM: slow

P.S.
• •

Quick is sometimes used instead of **quickly.** *Put out that fire quick!* But sometimes it would sound odd to use *quick* this way. You would not say "They quick saw that the bus had left." If you are not sure that *quick* sounds right, it is safer to use *quickly.*

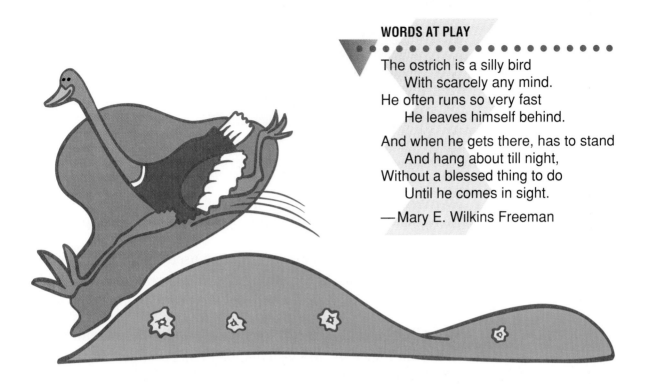

The ostrich is a silly bird
    With scarcely any mind.
He often runs so very fast
    He leaves himself behind.

And when he gets there, has to stand
    And hang about till night,
Without a blessed thing to do
    Until he comes in sight.

—Mary E. Wilkins Freeman

Listen to the seconds tick,
And you'll hear how time goes quick.
Listen for an hour or so,
And you'll know that time goes slow.

Remember
verb

Remember means to call something back to mind. *"Do you remember the name of the book you told me about?" asked Tim.*

Recall means to remember. It is often used when you make an effort to think of something. *I couldn't recall where I had left my glasses; then I realized they were on top of my head.*

Recollect means to recall something, especially something from long ago. *My grandmother can recollect her childhood as if it were yesterday.*

Think of can mean to remember. *I've met Harry's sister, but I can't think of her name.*

ANTONYM: forget

I couldn't **recall** where I had left my glasses; then I realized they were on top of my head.

Everyone at the party was **well-to-do** and wore expensive clothes.

Rich
adjective

Rich means having a lot of money or a lot of expensive things. *Samantha's grandfather owned a factory and became quite rich.*

Well-to-do means having enough money that you don't have to worry. *Everyone at the party was well-to-do and wore expensive clothes.*

Wealthy means very rich. *Two of Alicia's uncles became wealthy bankers.*

Made of money is an idiom that means very rich. It is mostly used in saying that someone is *not* rich. *She isn't made of money, you know, and can't afford a new car right now.*

ANTONYM: poor

The crowd watched the hot-air balloons **lift** into the sky.

Rise
verb

Rise means to get up or go up. *Carolina rose from her chair to open the door. When Aunt May gets mad, her voice rises.*

Arise means to get up, usually from a seat or a bed. It is a formal word. *Clara likes to arise before dawn.*

Ascend means to go upward steadily. *The plane ascended into the clouds and disappeared.*

Lift can mean to go up slowly. *The crowd watched the hot-air balloons lift into the sky.*

Soar means to fly at a great height or to fly upward. *The bird soared gracefully out of the canyon.*

SEE **ascend** for more words that mean to go up.
ANTONYM: fall

WORD STORY

Lift comes from a word meaning "air" in the language spoken by the Vikings. If you lift something, it goes up in the air.

Rough
adjective

Rough means having a surface that is not smooth. *All this gardening has made my hands rough and dry.*

Uneven means not smooth or level. *The plowed field was uneven and hard to walk across.*

Bumpy means having a lot of bumps. *The sidewalk is bumpy with snow and ice.*

Harsh means unpleasantly rough to the touch. *Sandpaper feels harsh if you rub your hand over it.*

Rugged means having a rough, uneven surface. *The mountain country was so rugged that once we even had to drive through a stream.*

ANTONYM: smooth

The mountain country was so **rugged** that once we even had to drive through a stream.

Run
verb

Run means to go fast by moving the legs quickly. *"Run after your father, Kumar, and tell him he forgot his lunch!" called his mother.*

SEE **hurry** for other words that mean to go fast.
SEE **walk** for words that mean to go on foot, but slower than running.

Run is also used in phrases that have special meanings. These phrases have their own sets of synonyms.

run away
run off

Run away and **run off** mean to leave very quickly because you want to get away. *"Tag, you're it!" yelled Maria and ran away. Then I tagged Sam and ran off too.*

Flee means almost the same as to run away. It can be used for running or for other ways of moving. *After the little clown squirted the big clown, he had to flee on a bicycle.*

Fly can mean to flee. *The soldiers tried to fly, but they were surrounded and taken prisoner.*

Escape means to get away from something. You escape quickly if you can, but you escape slowly if you have to. *The mouse dashed into its hole to escape the cat. The prisoners escaped by digging a tunnel.*

WORD POOL

Here are some words for different ways to move fast. They are not exact synonyms of *run,* but the actions they name are related. Use your dictionary to find their meanings.

bolt
dart
dash
gallop
jog
lope
race
scamper
scoot
scurry
sprint
trot

The mouse dashed into its hole to **escape** the cat.

Some of the phrases with **run** are not about moving fast.

run across
run into

Run across and **run into** mean to come face to face with someone or something, usually by chance. *I ran across Ms. Hill at the mall. It was the third time I'd run into her this week.*

Meet means to come face to face, usually by plan or for the first time. *"Meet me after school at the library," said Joseph. "I'd like you to meet my sister, Irena."*

Encounter is a formal word that means to run across. *Three days out of port, we encountered a pirate ship.*

Come across means to run across. It is generally used with things, not people. *I came across an old photo of Mom.*

run out of
run through

Run out of and **run through** mean to use up, so that none is left. *We ran out of milk before everyone had a glass, and we ran through the cookies soon afterward.*

Exhaust means to run out of. It is a formal word and suggests a lot of use. *The library has exhausted its money and cannot buy any more books this year.*

Consume means to use up in a steady way. *Homework and household chores consume most of my evenings.*

Drain can mean to use up. It suggests that there is a problem. *Illness can drain a family's budget.*

We **ran out of** milk before everyone had a glass, and we **ran through** the cookies soon afterward.

Sad
adjective

Sad means not happy or not pleased. *Reed made a sad face when he heard the bad news.*

Unhappy means sad. *The lion was very unhappy until the mouse pulled the thorn from his paw.*

Miserable means extremely unhappy. *Al is miserable about breaking his tape player.*

Sorry means sad, especially because of something you have done. *Nadine is sorry for what she said and wants to make friends again.*

Sorrowful and **mournful** mean full of sadness. *Lena had a sorrowful look on her face as she played the mournful tune.*

Downhearted means sad and discouraged. *Sally is downhearted about her bad grades.*

ANTONYM: happy

The lion was very **unhappy** until the mouse pulled the thorn from his paw.

The lion cubs felt **secure** close to their mother.

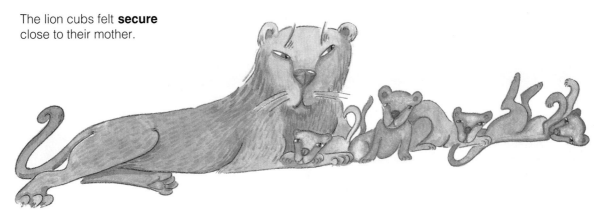

Safe
adjective

Safe means out of any danger. *LaTonya tries to stay safe on her bicycle by always wearing a helmet and following traffic rules.*

Secure means safe and without fear. *The lion cubs felt secure close to their mother.*

Protected means kept safe from danger. *Many of the ants are outside the ant hill, but the queen is protected inside.*

Snug means safe and comfortably protected. *The mountain lion keeps her cubs snug in their den.*

Out of harm's way is an idiom that means away from danger. *By the time the volcano erupted, the people were out of harm's way.*

ANTONYM: dangerous

WRITER'S CHOICE
● ●

When I am with Gigi, I feel secure and happy because I know I can share all my secrets with her, and she will understand.

—Nicholasa Mohr, *Going Home*

GOING HOME
Nicholasa Mohr

Why *secure*? Nicholasa Mohr uses *secure* to show that when this girl is with her friend, she feels safe and without fear.

Her friends **rescued** Amy before the sharks reached her.

Save
verb

Save means to make safe or to keep safe from danger. *The mayor saved the old building from being torn down.*

Rescue means to save with quick or strong actions. *Her friends rescued Amy before the sharks reached her.*

Deliver can mean to save from a danger or suffering. *A heavy rain delivered the town from the advancing forest fire.*

Reclaim means to save by bringing back to a good, useful condition. *The injured athlete reclaimed her skills through long workouts.*

Say
verb

Say means to put an idea or feeling into words. *"I'm ready," Mark said. What did Aunt Marilyn say in her postcard?*

Tell can mean to give information by speech or writing. *"Don't tell anyone where we're going, Leonard," whispered Judith. Does the poster tell what the movie is about?*

Voice means to say something, usually about your feelings. *Sandra often voices a strong dislike of insects.*

Declare can mean to say something firmly and openly. *"This is the best cake I ever ate," declared Ellis.*

State means to say something in a formal way. *The manager stated that the contest was over.*

Express means to say or to show exactly what you mean. *Jana's smile expressed her thanks for our help.*

SEE **talk** for words that mean to speak.

WRITING TIP: Writing Dialogue

You can sometimes use words such as *declare* or *state* instead of *say*. However, it is a good idea to use *say* most of the time. You may feel that you are repeating the word too often, but readers probably won't notice. If you use a lot of other words instead, readers probably will notice. If readers get interested in the words you use instead of the word *say*, they may not notice the rest of your writing.

Once in a while, a special word for *say* is exactly what you want. Here are some that you might use from time to time. These words are related, but they are not synonyms.

affirm	blurt	mention	proclaim	scream
announce	comment	mumble	remark	whisper
assert	cry	murmur	report	
assure	insist	mutter	relate	

Scare

verb

Scare means to make someone afraid. *It scares Jason when cars drive by too fast.*

Frighten means to fill someone with sudden fear. *Al's dog mask frightened the cat.*

Alarm means to cause worry about possible danger. *It alarms me if the phone rings late at night.*

Horrify means to make someone sick with fear. *It's horrifying to think that the plane nearly crashed.*

Terrify means to fill someone with very great fear. *The landslide terrified the climbers on the mountain.*

Make your flesh creep and **make your hair stand on end** are idioms that mean to scare you so much that you feel it all over your body. *The scary story that Mike told as we sat around the campfire made my flesh creep. Suddenly, a sharp noise behind us in the dark made my hair stand on end.*

SEE **afraid** for words that mean feeling fear.
SEE **fear** for words that mean the feeling of being afraid.
SEE **terrifying** for words that mean scary.

Al's dog mask **frightened** the cat.

"From this hill you can **see** for miles, Gabrielle," said her father.

See
verb

See means to know with your eyes. *"From this hill you can see for miles, Gabrielle," said her father.*

Behold means to see. It is an older word, often found in stories. *The weary and thirsty desert travelers beheld a lifesaving pool of water.*

Observe means to see and give attention to. *LeVon made notes on everything he observed in the bird's nest all month, then wrote them up as his science project.*

Notice means to observe. *"Notice how close to the ground that plane is flying, Agnes," said Mr. Dragovic.*

Perceive can mean to see and understand. It is a formal word. *"Do you perceive the difference between the shapes of those clouds?" asked Mrs. Flores.*

SEE **look** for words that mean to point your eyes at something.

The company **dispatched** a bicycle messenger with the package.

Send
verb

Send means to cause to move from one place to another. *Teams of scientists and engineers have sent rockets into outer space.*

Ship means to send by ship or some other vehicle. *Kasia shipped clothes and books in a trunk to her relatives in Poland.*

WORD STORY

Mail comes from an old French word meaning "bag," which is what mail is carried in.

Mail means to send by the post office and letter carriers. *"If you mail the invitations today, Wayne, they will arrive on Friday," said the postal clerk.*

Export means to send something out of the country to be sold in another country. *China exports silk garments to the United States.*

Transmit can mean to send signals or programs. *Weather forecasters transmit storm warnings by radio and TV.*

Dispatch means to send quickly. *The company dispatched a bicycle messenger with the package.*

ANTONYM: receive

Shape
noun

WORD POOL
• • • • • • • • •

Different shapes have their own names. How many of these shapes can you draw without using your dictionary? Look up the meanings of the ones you don't know.

circle
cone
cube
diamond
hexagon
octagon
oval
pentagon
pyramid
rectangle
sphere
square
triangle

Shape means the outward appearance of something, including its length, width, and thickness, but not its color or material. *Baseballs and softballs have the same round shape. The shape of a stop sign has eight sides. A shadow is only a shape.*

Form means a shape. *There's a snack shop in the form of a huge hot dog.*

Figure can mean a shape. *A figure with four equal sides is a square.*

Outline means a line that shows the shape of something. *When Sandar traced around his fingers with a pencil, he made an outline of his hand on the paper.*

Profile means a view of someone or something from one side, showing its shape. *Susan is good at drawing horses, but only in profile.*

Silhouette means a picture that is cut out of black paper. *Jamal could tell that it was a silhouette of Grandpa, with his high forehead and carefully trimmed beard.*

There's a snack shop in the **form** of a huge hot dog.

Shout

verb

WORD POOL

Here are other words meaning to speak loudly or to call out. Some are synonyms, and some are related words. Use your dictionary to help decide which are which.

bellow
cheer
groan
holler
howl
roar
screech
squawk
squeal
thunder
wail
whoop
yelp

Shout means to speak out in a loud voice to get the attention of someone. *Kate shouted, "I'm over here."*

Call means to speak in a louder voice than usual. *Ayako called to her friend on the front step next door.*

Yell means to shout as loud as you can when you are excited. *"That's my boy!" Mom yelled when Carlos hit a home run.*

Cry means to call out, with or without words. *When the ball hit Martin on the wrist, he cried, "Ow!"*

Scream means to cry out in a very loud voice. You scream when you are angry, afraid, or excited. *We all screamed when the roller coaster went down the steep slope.*

Shriek means to scream. *Shrieking with joy, the children ran into the ocean.*

SEE **loud** for words that mean with a big sound.
SEE **noise** for words that mean an unpleasant sound.

WORDS AT PLAY: Jump Rope Rhyme

Michael Jordan came to Duluth
To have a dentist pull his tooth
First he hollered, then he screamed,
Then he asked for some ice cream.

Our champion pumpkin was **displayed** at the county fair.

Show

verb

Show means to cause something to be seen. *Natalia showed her friends how well she could use her artificial hand.*

Display means to show things in a way that gets people's attention. *Our champion pumpkin was displayed at the county fair.*

Exhibit can mean to show something publicly. *On Visitors' Day, the school classes exhibit drawings they have done.*

Expose can mean to show openly where anyone can see. *When the wall of the building was torn down, the rooms inside were all exposed.*

Point out means to show where something is or to call attention to something. *Rosita pointed out the rabbit hiding in the bush.*

ANTONYMS: conceal, hide

Shut
verb

Shut means to close. *"Shut your eyes and go to sleep, Jesse!" said his grandfather; then he shut the bedroom door quietly.*

Shut is also used in phrases that have special meanings. Each of these phrases has a different set of synomyms.

shut down

Shut down means to stop the activities of a business or other organization. *The park's softball league shuts down in the fall and starts again in spring.*

Close can mean to shut down permanently. *The Kims closed their grocery store and opened a restaurant.*

shut in

Shut in means to keep someone or something from going out. *The cows are shut in at night.*

Enclose means to shut in with a wall or something like a wall. *High buildings enclose the park.*

Imprison means to put in prison or in something like a prison. *Jenny imprisoned the beetle in a jar for two days, then let it go.*

The cows are **shut in** at night.

The curtains in Lia's bedroom **shut out** the light from the street lamp.

shut out

Shut out means to keep someone or something from coming in. *The curtains in Lia's bedroom shut out the light from the street lamp.*

Exclude means to shut out. It is a formal word. *City law excludes factories from this neighborhood.*

Bar means to shut out by a lock or as if by a lock. *That store bars anyone without shoes.*

shut up

Shut up means to make or become quiet. *Tony shut up when the principal walked into the room.*

Hush means to make someone or something quiet. *The mother hushed her crying baby in the back of the church.*

Silence means to make someone or something completely quiet. *The sight of the cat silenced the birds.*

P.S.

● ●

Some of these phrases have other meanings, too:

Shut up can mean to seal something that will not be used for a while. *The city shuts up the ice-skating rink after Easter.*

Shut out can mean to keep an opposing team from scoring at all. *The Jets shut out the Aces, 4 to 0.*

Shy
adjective

Shy means lacking confidence and uneasy in the presence of others. *Shy people feel uncomfortable talking to strangers.*

Bashful means shy and easily embarrassed. *Martha was so bashful that she wouldn't even look at George.*

Timid means shy and frightened. *Butch is a timid child, but he made a good speech at the school assembly.*

Modest can mean unwilling to draw attention to yourself. *Shayne is so modest that she lets other people get the praise for her work.*

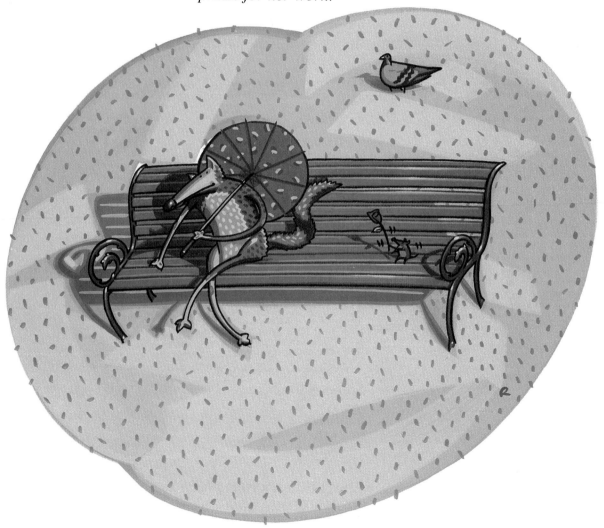

Martha was so **bashful** that she wouldn't even look at George.

The turtle is so **slow** that it takes hours to cross the yard.

Slow
adjective

Slow means taking a long time to go or do or happen. *The turtle is so slow that it takes hours to cross the yard. Joe did a slow and careful job with no mistakes.*

Leisurely means relaxed and without hurry. *"Let's go to the park and have a nice leisurely picnic," suggested Mom.*

Poky means slow and without energy. *Ruby's poky dog never wants to play.*

Sluggish means slow and tired. *I am so sluggish in the morning that I often nearly miss the bus.*

ANTONYMS: fast, quick

P.S.

Slow is sometimes used instead of **slowly.** *Drive slow near the school.* But sometimes it would sound odd to use *slow* this way. You would not say "Slow I learned to twirl a baton." If you are not sure that *slow* sounds right, it is best to use *slowly.*

The **smart** puppy figured out how to open the gate.

Smart
adjective

WORD STORY
• • • • • • • • • • • • • •
Alert comes from Italian words meaning "on watch." Soldiers who keep watch have to stay alert.

Smart means able to learn easily and solve problems quickly. *The smart puppy figured out how to open the gate.*

Intelligent means able to think clearly and make good decisions. *"It is intelligent of you to get your work done early so you'll have time left to play, Rosemary," said Mrs. Gregoris.*

Alert can mean very quick to understand and to respond. *The alert bus driver slowed down right away when she saw ice on the road ahead.*

Clever means quick to think of good ideas. *The clever boy had a plan for the Native American Day program.*

Bright can mean smart in an active way. *César is bright, so he enjoys puzzles and riddles.*

Brainy means very smart. It is an informal word. *"If you're so brainy, how come you always lose your glasses?" asked Sandy's brother.*

ANTONYM: stupid

Smooth
adjective

Smooth means having a surface with no roughness or uneven spaces. *"Is Ron's baseball the new, smooth one?" asked Tom.*

Polished means made smooth and shiny by rubbing with a cloth. *Angelica's grandmother keeps all their furniture clean and brightly polished.*

Silky means smooth and shiny like silk. *This shampoo promises to make your hair as silky as a baby's.*

Slippery means so smooth that it causes slipping. *When Anne saw that the floor had just been washed, she knew it would be slippery.*

Slick means smooth. It can also mean slippery. *Tran's father drove slowly because the rain made the roads slick.*

ANTONYMS: bumpy, rough, uneven

WORD STORY

Silky comes from a Greek word meaning "Chinese." The Chinese were the first people to make silk.

WRITING TIP: Comparing Things

One way to make your writing interesting is to use comparisons. For example, a writer wanting to show the smoothness of ice might use the following comparison:

The ice was hard and gleaming, like polished marble.

Sometimes writers make comparisons without using *like* or *as:*

The frog was a piece of slippery soap that no one could hold on to.

The words in this book, and the sentences with them, will help you think of comparisons and how to write them.

Soft
adjective

Soft means tender, not hard or stiff. *Josh closed the bread bag so that the bread would stay fresh and soft.*

Many words that mean **soft** compare things to some other soft material.

Fluffy means as soft as fluff. *The young swan has short fluffy feathers.*

Fleecy means as soft as sheep's wool. *The fleecy collar on Shalonda's coat felt comfortable.*

Spongy means soft and absorbent, like a sponge. *Eagle Calls wasn't hurt when he fell on the spongy moss.*

Mushy means as soft and wet as mush. *After the storm the soccer field will be mushy.*

Silky means as soft and smooth as silk. *Inez showed Aunt Rosa her silky new party dress.*

SEE **smooth** for words that mean having a surface with no roughness.
ANTONYM: hard

WORDS FROM WORDS

soft
softball
soft-boiled
soften
softener
softheaded
softhearted
soft-shelled
soft-spoken
software
softwood
softy

The young swan has short **fluffy** feathers.

The space shuttle flight **starts** with the roar of powerful engines.

Start
verb

Start means to set something going. *The space shuttle flight starts with the roar of powerful engines.*

Begin means to start something, or to start doing something. *Julie began her letter, "Dear Grandma." The snow began to fall around midnight.*

Commence means to start. It is a formal word. *My sister's graduation ceremony commences at ten o'clock.*

Get going means to begin. *"It's time to get going on your homework, Lucille," said her dad.*

Lead off means to start something. *Jan led off story time by telling about her favorite animal.*

ANTONYMS: finish, stop

The police officer held up his hand and **halted** traffic.

Stop
verb

Stop means to keep from doing or happening. *"Stop your arguing this minute!" said an exasperated Mrs. Hockett. If Ed wants to stop gaining weight, he has to eat less and exercise more.*

Halt means to force to stop for a time. *The police officer held up his hand and halted traffic.*

Prevent means to stop. *Ropes prevented the crowd from getting too close to the rock group.*

Cease means to stop something that has gone on for a while. *The branch was too high, so Stavros finally ceased his efforts to reach the apple.*

Discontinue means to stop something that has been happening for a long time. *They've discontinued the Happy Howard Harmonica Hour, my favorite TV show!*

Interrupt means to stop something in the middle. *The threat of lightning interrupted Manuella's little league game.*

Check means to stop suddenly and forcefully, if only for a short time. *The fence checked the dog's escape until it dug a hole and got out.*

SEE **end** for words that mean to reach the last part.
SEE **last** for words that mean final.
ANTONYMS: begin, start

Story

noun

WORD POOL

There are many different kinds of stories you might like to read—or write. Use your dictionary to find out the differences.

- **autobiography**
- **ballad**
- **biography**
- **epic**
- **fable**
- **fairy tale**
- **folklore**
- **legend**
- **mystery**
- **myth**
- **novel**
- **parable**
- **romance**
- **science fiction**
- **western**

Story means a set of events, told in words. *My sister Dyan told me a scary story. "Do you want Dave to write a story about you?" asked Allyson.*

Tale means a story, usually of imaginary events. *Pearl loves her grandfather's tales of princesses, treasures, and long voyages.*

Yarn can mean a long story that goes on and on, about unbelievable events. *My little sister Melissa believes that Uncle Earl's yarn about the pretty mermaid and the great blue whale is a true story.*

Narrative means the same as story. It is a formal word. *Every narrative has a beginning, a middle, and an end.*

Pearl loves her grandfather's **tales** of princesses, treasures, and long voyages.

Piano movers have to be very **strong**.

Strong
adjective

Strong means having great power or strength. *Piano movers have to be very strong.*

Powerful means full of power and force. *Six powerful horses pull the heavy wagon. "Don't take too much of this powerful medicine," warned Dr. Jamison.*

Sturdy means strong and solidly built. *Be sure that the ladder is sturdy before you climb up to the roof.*

Stout can mean sturdy. *The stout walls of the cabin kept the pioneers safe and warm.*

Tough can mean strong and able to resist wear and tear. *Shoes made of tough leather will last a long time.*

Robust means strong and healthy. *The robust campers filled their days with sports and games.*

Hardy means strong enough and healthy enough to overcome all difficulties. *This will be Donny's first plant, so let's get him a hardy one that doesn't need much care.*

ANTONYM: weak

WORD STORY

Robust comes from a Latin word meaning "oak." Oak trees are often big and strong, like a healthy person.

Stupid
adjective

Stupid means very slow to learn or understand. *I felt stupid when I couldn't remember my own phone number.*

Dull can mean not quick to think, learn, or act. *Why am I always so dull when I wake up?*

Slow can mean dull. *We thought the puppy was going to be slow, but he just needed time to get used to us.*

Dumb can mean stupid and silly. *It was kind of dumb of me to leave the birdcage door open.*

Dense can mean stupid. *She gets a dense expression when she is thinking really hard about her computer.*

ANTONYMS: intelligent, smart

I felt **stupid** when I couldn't remember my own phone number.

Suddenly
adverb

Suddenly means quickly and without being expected. *Suddenly Amie sneezed and gave away her hiding place. We were scared when the lights went out suddenly.*

Unexpectedly means without any sign that something is going to happen. *The clown's mirror unexpectedly squirted water into the other clown's face.*

Abruptly means suddenly. *Mom stopped the car abruptly to avoid hitting the raccoon.*

Short can mean suddenly. *The jogger stopped short when the dog charged at him.*

Instantly means at once, without delay. *Roger jumped on the trampoline and instantly bounced up again.*

Immediately means instantly. *When Nan caught the basketball, she immediately shot a basket.*

Pronto is an informal word that means right now, as fast as you can. *"Get those dishes washed pronto!" Jim said, as we all rushed to get ready to leave.*

All of a sudden means suddenly. *All of a sudden Roberto stopped talking to hear the new song on the radio.*

All at once means suddenly. *All at once the geese flew up.*

SEE **quick** for words that mean fast.
ANTONYM: gradually

WORD STORY

Pronto comes from a Spanish word meaning "quickly." People used the Spanish word so much that it became a word in the English language too.

All at once the geese flew up.

Clara is **sure** that she saw a strange animal in the forest.

Sure
adjective

WORDS FROM WORDS

● ● ● ● ● ● ● ● ● ●

assure
assuredly
insurance
insure
reassurance
reassure
sure
surefire
surefooted
surely
unsure

Sure means having no doubt. *Clara is sure that she saw a strange animal in the forest.*

Confident means sure, with a hopeful feeling. *Ariel is confident that with practice her reading will improve.*

Positive means sure, without any second thoughts. *Melanie is positive that she is the fastest runner in her class, because she wins every race.*

Certain means sure, based on the facts. *Running Deer was certain that George Washington was the first President of the United States.*

ANTONYMS: doubtful, uncertain

Surprise
verb

Surprise means to fill someone with wonder because of something unexpected. *We plan to surprise Linda with a birthday party.*

Astonish and **amaze** mean to surprise someone greatly. *The magician astonished the children by making the parrot vanish. Next, he amazed them with a card trick.*

Astound means to surprise someone completely, so that the person has trouble understanding what has happened. *It's astounding that a ten-year-old won the chess tournament.*

Startle means to make someone jump in surprise and fright. *The door slammed and startled Ms. Mackay.*

WRITER'S CHOICE

As she entered his yard Saburo often came to greet her, and she would call out, "Spread your tail, Saburo, spread your tail!" And sometimes he would surprise her by making an enormous multi-colored fan of himself.

—Yoshiko Uchida, *Sumi & the Goat & the Tokyo Express*

Why *surprise?* Yoshiko Uchida uses *surprise* to show that although Sumi asks Saburo, the peacock, to spread his tail, she does not really expect him to do it. When he does, it fills her with wonder.

"And sometimes he would **surprise** her by making an enormous multi-colored fan of himself."

Take
verb

Take means to make something your own or to get hold of something. *"Here, take my chair," said Craig. Rod likes to take Gramp's hand when they walk.*

Take is also used in phrases that have special meanings. Each of these phrases has its own set of synonyms.

take down

Take down means to write something so that you can remember it. *Tim took down the coach's speech for the school paper.*

Note means almost the same as to take down. It suggests writing in a shorter form. *When Pedro goes to a baseball game, he notes the names of the players who get hits.*

Jot means to write quickly. *Belle jotted a shopping list on the back of an envelope.*

Record means to put something in writing or any other permanent form. It is a formal word. *This monument records the names of Americans who died in the war.*

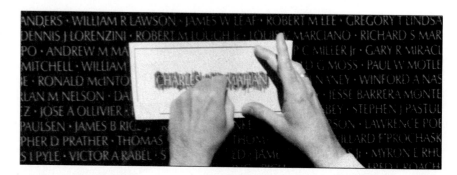

This monument **records** the names of Americans who died in the war.

take in
                                                         Take in means to receive, especially as part of business. *The new after-school program takes in kids from two neighborhoods.*

Admit can mean to allow to enter. *My ticket to the fair said "Admit One."*

Accept can mean to receive with approval. *The magazine has accepted my poem!*

Welcome can mean to receive gladly. *Rocco's soccer team welcomes new players.*

take on
                                                          Take on means to give someone a job. *That store takes on extra salespeople during the holidays.*

Hire means to take on. *Some companies hire people with disabilities first.*

Employ means to hire. It suggests a steady job. *Mr. Kim's dry-cleaning business employs six people now.*

Engage can mean the same as to employ. It is a formal word. *If I were a millionaire, I would engage a butler and a driver and a cook and a gardener.*

P.S.
• •
Some of these phrases have other meanings, too:

Take down and **take off** can mean to remove something. *Momma takes down the heavy curtains and takes off the blankets when it gets warm.*

Take in can mean to understand. *I couldn't take in what Stella was telling me.* **Take in** can also mean to fool someone. *His story about living in Alaska took me in completely.*

Take on can mean to agree to do some work. *Alma is old enough to take on some jobs around the house.*

Talk
verb

Louise often **chats** with her friend Trish on the phone.

Talk means to make words with your voice. *The fire chief talked about fire safety.*

Speak means to say words. *Rita speaks often of how much she liked the class trip to the museum.*

Chat means to talk with others in a light, friendly way. *Louise often chats with her friend Trish on the phone.*

Discuss means to talk about something, hearing several opinions. *We discussed a plan for collecting glass, tin cans, and newspapers.*

Debate can mean to discuss something in a formal way, with each person taking a turn to speak and reply. *The candidates debated the state's budget plan.*

SEE **argue** for words that mean to fight with words.
SEE **say** for words that mean to put something into words.

P.S.

Talk is used in some phrases that have entered our language only in the last 30 years:

A **talk show** is a television program in which a host chats with mostly famous people.

A **talking head** is a close-up television picture, from the shoulders up, of someone talking.

Talk radio is a radio program of live telephone conversations with listeners.

During our camping trip there was a **terrible** rainstorm.

Terrible

adjective

Terrible means very bad. *During our camping trip there was a terrible rainstorm.*

Awful can mean very bad or unpleasant. *Donna has to stay home today because of her awful cold.*

Nasty can mean very unpleasant. *Felipe got a nasty scrape when he fell off his bike, but it's not serious.*

Horrible can mean very bad or foul. *A horrible smell was coming from the garbage truck ahead of us.*

Rotten can mean extremely bad. *I practice, but I'm rotten at video games.*

Horrid can mean extremely bad or unpleasant. *Today the food at school was really horrid.*

SEE **bad** for words that mean a bit better than terrible.
ANTONYMS: great, wonderful

Terrifying

adjective

Terrifying means causing great fear. *A terrifying storm blew down trees and tore roofs off houses.*

Horrifying means causing great fear and disgust. *Our neighborhood was shocked by news of the horrifying accident.*

Scary means likely to scare you. *Evan is watching a really scary movie.*

Frightening means likely to scare you very badly. *It is frightening to think that Grandpa is going to the hospital.*

Frightful means frightening. *A frightful scream in the dark scared the young campers.*

Dreadful means causing fear. *A dreadful dragon prowls this forest.*

SEE **afraid** for words that mean how you feel when something terrifying happens.
SEE **fear** for words that mean the feeling of being afraid.
SEE **scare** for words that mean to make someone afraid.

Evan is watching a really **scary** movie.

Thin

adjective

Thin means not having much flesh. *Umberto is so thin that he can squeeze through the narrow gate.*

Lean means not fat. *The lost dog was lean and hungry.*

Slender means pleasingly thin. *The slender dancer looked very graceful.*

Slim means slender. *The slim cowgirl mounted her horse.*

Lanky means tall and thin and awkward-looking. *The lanky, long-armed pitcher threw very hard pitches.*

Skinny means too thin. *The runner looks skinny, but he wins almost every race.*

All skin and bones is an idiom that means very thin. *After being sick for a month, and losing twenty pounds, my brother was all skin and bones.*

ANTONYM: fat

WORDS AT PLAY

There was a young lady from Lynn
Who was so exceedingly thin
    That when she essayed
    To drink lemonade
She slid down the straw and fell in!

WRITING TIP: Suggested Meanings

When you choose words, you must think of what a word means and of what else the word suggests. For example, *slender* and *skinny* both mean thin. *Slender* suggests a pleasing slimness. *Skinny* suggests that someone or something is too thin.

Thing

noun

Thing means any single part of all there is. If it's not a person or a place or an action, it's a thing. *All sorts of things were available at the Jacksons' yard sale.*

Object means a thing that can be seen or touched. *Jean came home from the outing with rocks, shells, leaves, and all sorts of other objects.*

Article can mean a particular thing, and often means a thing of a certain kind. *Pedro has a collection of metal soldiers, model ships, and other military articles.*

Item means a thing that is part of a group or list. *"Will every item on our shopping list fit in the cart?" wondered Mom.*

All sorts of **things** were available at the Jacksons' yard sale.

Be careful not to overuse the word *thing* in your writing. Sometimes *thing* is the right word; for example, if you want to picture a strange, unknown creature:

A huge, green, slimy thing emerged from the spaceship.

Many times, *thing* is the wrong word; for example, if you want to give a clear picture of how a machine works:

This thing sends oil through these other things, into this round thing with a thing in it that moves back and forth.

Think

verb

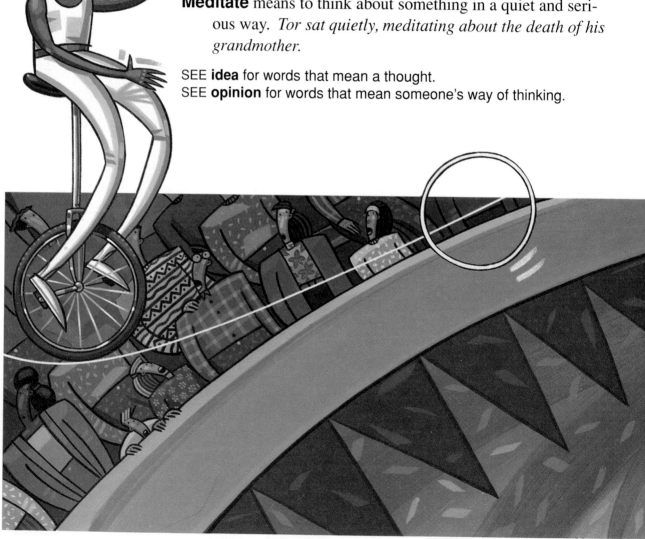

Think means to use the mind in order to form ideas or understand something. *Gramps is thinking about living with us so he won't have to climb stairs.*

Reason means to think carefully in order to make a judgment or solve a problem. *Tanya reasoned her way through the difficult test.*

Concentrate can mean to pay special attention and think really hard. *The acrobat must concentrate to do this trick.*

Meditate means to think about something in a quiet and serious way. *Tor sat quietly, meditating about the death of his grandmother.*

SEE **idea** for words that mean a thought.
SEE **opinion** for words that mean someone's way of thinking.

The acrobat must **concentrate** to do this trick.

Throw
verb

Throw means to make something go through the air by moving your arm and hand. *The acrobat's helper throws hoops up for him to juggle.*

Toss means to throw easily or gently. *Ralph tossed the beachball to his little brother.*

Fling means to throw something forcefully without caring just where it goes. *The baby often flings her toys around.*

Hurl means to fling. *The giant picked up a rock and hurled it down the mountainside.*

Pitch means to throw something and try to make it go to a certain place. *Maeve pitched in the softball game yesterday and her friend Eulalie caught. We are pitching snowballs at that tree trunk.*

Heave can mean to throw, especially something that is heavy. *Mr. Short Bull heaved the suitcase into the trunk of his car.*

The acrobat's helper **throws** hoops up for him to juggle.

P.S.
• •
Throw is used in phrases that have special meanings:

Throw away means to get rid of things. *Ron threw away the old rags he found in the closet.*

Throw in means to add. *The baker throws in an extra roll when we buy a dozen.*

Throw off means to get rid of someone or a group. *The cattle rustlers threw off the posse by riding through the stream.*

Throw out can mean to cause to leave. *The umpire threw the angry player out of the game.*

Tiny
adjective

Tiny means very small. *Uncle Fritz wears a tiny hearing aid in his left ear.*

Teeny means tiny. *A teeny ladybug landed on Amy's shoulder.*

Minute means very tiny. It is pronounced mī nüt′. *A minute speck of dust can float in the air without being seen.*

Miniature means very much smaller than usual. *The dollhouse in the museum has miniature clocks and miniature furniture.*

Microscopic means so tiny that it can be seen only by using a microscope. *These microscopic living things can be clearly seen when they are magnified.*

Itty-bitty and **itsy-bitsy** mean tiny. They are informal words. *"Help me find the itty-bitty screw that fell out of my eyeglasses, Leonora," said her grandfather "It goes in this itsy-bitsy hole."*

SEE **little** for words that mean small, but bigger than tiny.
ANTONYMS: gigantic, huge

These **microscopic** living things can be clearly seen when they are magnified.

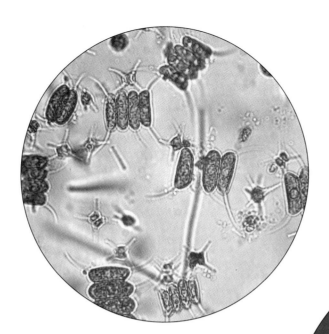

These are enlarged pictures of **microscopic** living things.

After working in their garden, the kids were **tired.**

Tired
adjective

Tired means having little energy or strength left. *After working in their garden, the kids were tired.*

Weary means very tired and unable to do more. *Mom was weary after working all day.*

Exhausted can mean having no strength or energy left at all. *At the end of 20 miles, the hikers were too exhausted to go on.*

Worn-out can mean exhausted. *The worn-out runners barely made it to the end of the long race.*

Sleepy means tired and ready to sleep. *Juanita gets sleepy about 9 o'clock.*

Tool
noun

Tool means something used to make work easier, especially something used by hand. *The kids picked up their gardening tools and walked home.*

Device means a tool used for a special job. *A tongue depressor is a device a doctor uses to examine your throat.*

Instrument means a tool used for a special job that requires exactness. *Dr. Melos used several instruments when she gave me a complete examination.*

Utensil means a tool, especially one used in cooking. *"Which utensil works best for whipping cream?" asked Carl.*

Gadget means a small, convenient tool or machine. *My father bought a new gadget to clean his teeth with.*

Appliance means a machine that does a particular job, especially in the home. *Mr. Soon has a business repairing toasters, lamps, and other small appliances.*

The kids picked up their gardening **tools** and walked home.

After reaching the peak, the mountain climbers began the hard **trek** back.

Trip
noun

Trip means the act of going some distance. *Lynn's family went on a trip to Long Beach.*

Journey means a long trip. *Ms. Koehler spent her vacation on a journey through the desert.*

Tour means a trip, often to see many places. *The zookeeper gave Cory a tour of the zoo.*

Voyage means a long trip, especially by ship. *Les is reading about famous people who made voyages across the Atlantic.*

Cruise means a voyage for pleasure that takes you to several places. *We will visit four islands on our sea cruise.*

Expedition means a trip for some special purpose. *Expeditions into space use special equipment.*

Outing means a short trip for enjoyment. *The Rosarios have a picnic outing planned for Saturday.*

Trek means a long and difficult trip. *After reaching the peak, the mountain climbers began the hard trek back.*

Ms. Koehler spent her vacation on a **journey** through the desert.

Expeditions into space use special equipment.

We will visit four islands on our sea **cruise**.

Turn
verb

Turn means to go around like a wheel. *When the fan turns, it makes a breeze.*

Revolve means to go in a curve around some place. *Earth revolves around the sun once every year.*

Rotate means to turn around a central point. *Earth rotates on its axis every day.*

Spin means to turn quickly. *The figure skater spins in a graceful twirl.*

Wheel means to turn quickly and gracefully. *The shortstop wheeled and threw to second base.*

The figure skater **spins** in a graceful twirl.

P.S.

Turn is used in phrases that have special meanings:

Turn down can mean to refuse an offer. *Aki was so full that he turned down a second helping of stew.*

Turn in can mean to give back or to exchange something. *Mom wants to turn in our old car and get a smaller one.*

Turn out can mean to happen or to become known. *It turns out in Chapter 5 that the dentist is really a spy.*

Turn up can mean to appear or to be found. *Clyde's missing sock turned up in the dirty laundry.*

Ugly
adjective

Ugly means very unpleasant to look at. *A soccer ball hit me in the face and caused an ugly purple swelling.*

Unsightly means ugly. It is a milder word. *An unsightly rusty gutter hung from the roof.*

Hideous means very ugly and horrible to look at. *A hideous troll kept people from crossing the bridge by making faces at them.*

Unattractive means not likely to attract people because of an appearance that is not pleasant. *The house is unattractive to possible buyers because it is so dirty.*

ANTONYMS: beautiful, pretty, handsome

A **hideous** troll kept people from crossing the bridge by making faces at them.

Very

adverb

Very means much more than usual. *After the storm, it became very hot. With binoculars, you can see very far.*

Awfully, dreadfully, and **terribly** can mean truly and deeply. *We walked an awfully long way and were dreadfully tired— but we were all terribly glad to be home!*

Extremely and **exceedingly** mean greatly. *Mr. Stratas was extremely happy to have his lost wallet returned. He was exceedingly unhappy about losing it.*

Highly means fully and actively. *Suraya is highly pleased with the school's new computer class.*

Mighty can mean very. Used this way, it is an informal word. *We were mighty glad to see land again after four days in a drifting boat.*

With binoculars, you can see **very** far.

The word *very* is often overused. See what happens in the paragraph below when we replace *very* with more precise words.

An Exceedingly

A Very Steep Trail

extremely

The Rocky Mountains are very tall.

When you hike in the mountains, you can see

an awfully   highly

a very long way down. It is very thrilling to be

mighty

so very high up. We felt very proud of ourselves

for walking that far. Climbing a mountain is

terribly

a very exciting adventure.

Walk

verb

Walk means to move on foot. *Carol and Sheila spent an hour walking around the mall.*

Step means to walk, especially a short distance. *Julio stepped over to the fountain for a drink of water.*

Pace means to walk back and forth. *Max paced the platform, waiting for the subway train.*

March means to walk steadily, with a regular step. *Bands march to the beat of drums.*

Stride means to take long steps. *Scott strode along the side-walk, trying to keep up with his older brother.*

Shuffle means to walk without taking your feet from the ground. *Tonya carefully shuffled her way across the icy bridge.*

Plod means to walk slowly and heavily. *The tired puppy plodded along behind us.*

SEE the Word Pool at **run** for words that mean to move your feet fast.

The tired puppy
plodded along
behind us.

I watched as Peaches shuffled along the gate toward the entrance to the ball field.

—Walter Dean Myers, *Me, Mop, and the Moondance Kid*

Why *shuffled?* Peaches is a tramp. Walter Dean Myers uses *shuffled* to show that Peaches has very little energy, not even enough to pick his feet up off the ground.

WORD POOL

There are lots of different ways to walk. Use your dictionary to look up the meaning of several of these words. Your friends can look up other words from the list. Then you can take turns moving around the room in the ways that your words describe.

amble	stalk
clump	stamp
hike	stroll
hobble	strut
limp	stumble
lumber	swagger
lurch	tiptoe
pad	totter
prance	tramp
saunter	tread
shamble	trip
stagger	trudge

Want

verb

Want means to have or feel a need for something. *Everyone wants to have friends.*

Wish means to hope for something. *Lloyd wished he could find his lost watch.*

Desire means to want very much. It is a formal word. *People all over the world desire peace.*

Crave means to want something greatly. *Kay craves ice cream, and she never gets enough of it.*

Have your heart set on is an idiom that means to wish for something very much. *Ruben has his heart set on going to visit his cousins this summer.*

WORDS AT PLAY

• • • • • • • • • • • • • • • • •

A diner while dining at Crewe,
Found quite a large mouse in his stew.
　　Said the waiter, "Don't shout
　　And wave it about,
Or the rest will be wanting one, too."

Wet

adjective

Wet means covered with water or full of water. *"It's too cold for you to go outside with wet hair, Kristin," said her mother.*

Soaked means thoroughly wet from being in water for a while. *Our tent blew over in the storm and we got soaked.*

Soggy means heavy with water. *After I dry the dishes, the towel is all soggy.*

Drenched means completely wet. *The drenched puppy shivered when he came in the house.*

Soaking wet and **dripping wet** mean completely wet. *"Come out of the rain before you get soaking wet, Oscar!" called Mrs. Landerback. "But leave that dripping wet umbrella outside."*

SEE **damp** for words that mean only a little bit wet.
ANTONYM: dry

WORD POOL

These words are not synonyms for wet, but they are names of different places where you could get very wet. Use your dictionary to find the meanings of these words.

bay	creek	pool	sound
bayou	gulf	puddle	swamp
bog	lagoon	river	waterfall
brook	lake	sea	whirlpool
canal	marsh	spring	
channel	ocean	stream	
cove	pond	strait	

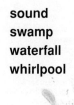

Wicked

adjective

Wicked means doing wrong things on purpose. *The wicked men forced children to work in dangerous factories.*

Bad can mean wicked. *Hurting an animal is a very bad thing to do.*

Immoral means doing things that people agree are very wrong. *Cheating people to get their money is immoral.*

Evil means wicked and causing great harm. *The evil queen wilted the flowers with her stare.*

SEE **naughty** for words that mean behaving badly.
ANTONYM: good

The **evil** queen wilted the flowers with her stare.

When the athletes came out, the crowd went **wild.**

Wild

adjective

WORD STORY

● ● ● ● ● ● ● ● ● ● ●

Savage comes from a Latin word meaning "forest." Because many forest animals are fierce and ready to fight, *savage* got that meaning.

Wild means extremely excited and out of control. *When the athletes came out, the crowd went wild.*

Raging means out of control because of anger. *The raging elephant will not let the zookeepers near her baby.*

Savage can mean fierce and ready to fight. *At night that store is guarded by a savage dog.*

Unruly means hard to control. *"If this class gets any more unruly, everyone will get extra homework," warned Mrs. Kirby.*

Beside yourself is an idiom that means too wild to think. *She is beside herself because she lost her wallet with more than fifty dollars in it.*

SEE **mad** for words that mean angry.
SEE **naughty** for words that mean behaving badly.
ANTONYMS: calm, peaceful

Work

noun

Work means effort in doing or making something. *Washing the car is an hour's work for Jon.*

Labor means work that takes a lot of strength. *Putting up a building requires much human labor and skill.*

Toil means long and tiring work. *After days of toil, the bird completed its nest.*

Industry can mean steady, hard work. *The children showed such industry in cleaning the basement that Mrs. Oliva took them all to a movie.*

Elbow grease is an idiom that means hard work, especially physical work. *It will take plenty of elbow grease to get all those shelves clean.*

SEE **job** for words that mean something that has to be done.
ANTONYM: play

Putting up a building requires much human **labor** and skill.

Resources

An essay on being creative, a writer's guide, and complete indexes

Being Creative

Everyone is creative. You create something every time you have an idea. When you say something you haven't said before, you've created a sentence. You're creative when you play make-believe games or when you daydream! If you make a new joke, whistle a new tune, or even think of a new sandwich—you're creative!

Getting More Creative

Creativity is a great thing to have and to use. And it gets better the more you use it. People practice the piano or practice a sport to get better. You can practice being creative to get better at that too. Try these ideas. Think of them as mind exercise.

THOUGHTS FROM EVERYWHERE

If you have a question to answer, try choosing an answer by chance. Suppose your question is, "What am I going to do for my science project?" Try this: open this book to any page, close your eyes, and touch any word on that page. What's the word? Think of a way to use that word to answer your question. For example, if the word is *bird,* your project could be listing kinds of birds you see this week.

THOUGHTS TOGETHER

Take two words from different pages of this book. Can you connect the two ideas? Can you use the words to help you decide something? Suppose you're wondering what to do on Saturday. Can the words help you come up with an idea?

NEW AND DIFFERENT THOUGHTS

Try thinking about things in new ways. Pick the name of something from any page of this book. Make up a new game you could play with that thing. Suppose the word is *apple*. The game could be to balance an apple on your head while you walk across a room. What other games can you think of using an apple?

CREATIVITY TIPS

You can exercise your creativity by doing things differently from your normal way. Try walking to school a different way every morning next week. When you watch television, watch programs you don't usually watch. Lie on your bedroom floor for ten minutes. Think about how it would be if the room really were upside down. Would you tie yourself into bed on the ceiling every night?

Imagine what the world is like for animals. A dog tells more by smell than by sight. If you close your eyes, how many smells can you notice? What do they tell you? How many times can you tell where you are just by smell?

If you were a mouse, what would the grass look like to you? To a mouse the grass is probably as big as a jungle. Imagine what it would be like if you were that small, and you lived in the grass or in a garden.

Writing Creatively

Writing is a very creative activity. We're creative in just about everything that we write—stories, poems, journal entries, even school reports.

Nonfictional writing is creative too. The creative part is how the author puts the facts together to make the writing interesting. In the paragraph below, the author describes an ant (called Lasius flavus) in a rain shower. How does she make the facts interesting?

> *"She was lost on a prairie of cement. The wind blew, raindrops splashed and formed little lakes. The lakes joined together and created a sea. Lasius flavus climbed up on a matchstick. The sea became an ocean, the matchstick a boat."*

—from *All Upon a Sidewalk* by Jean Craighead George

To make the facts interesting and to help us understand what it's like to be an ant in a rain shower, Jean Craighead George compares this shower to a storm at sea. Imagining a storm at sea helps you to understand how a rain shower might feel to an ant.

Writing Tips

You can exercise your own creativity and find new and interesting ideas to use in your own writing. Here are some simple ways. Add your own ideas to this list.

WRITE WHAT YOU SEE AND HEAR
Keep a journal. Write down the interesting things you see and hear. When you think of something interesting or funny of your own, write it down. Carry your journal with you so you can write things down while you still remember them.

WRITE WHAT YOU READ
Use your journal to write down interesting things that you read. If you like a poem or a joke or a way of describing something, write it down. You'll come up with your own ideas from these things that you've read.

WRITE WHAT YOU IMAGINE
If something interests you, imagine doing it yourself and then write what you imagined in your journal. Have you ever put yourself into a story you were reading? What did you do when you were in the story? Have you ever wondered about characters in a movie

or a book—what were their lives like before the movie or book started, or after it ended?

PLAY WRITING GAMES

Get together with a friend. Each of you can start a story or a poem. Then you can trade and write some of each other's. Then change again. Try this one: what would you write as the second line of this limerick? Have a friend write the third line. Keep going until you've finished the limerick.

There once was a cowboy named Tony

How do you think this story goes on?

After the lion escaped from the zoo, the police chased it into the library.

Tips on Getting Started

Sometimes you want to write something, and you don't know what to write about or how to get started. Try using a little creativity to help you think of things. These ideas might help you get started:

PLAY WITH WORDS

Pick a word and think of two or three words that rhyme with it. Write a poem that uses them all.

START A STORY

Take a book, any book. Open it to any page, put your finger down, and start a story with the sentence you touch. Pretend somebody is saying it.

"Many oranges and grapefruits are grown in Florida," said the mysterious lady in the black dress.

What is the rest of the story?

WRITE FROM A DRAWING

Make a drawing of a person and tell a story about the drawing. Think about questions like these: Why does this person look this way? Where is he or she from? How old is the person? What does he or she like?

MAKE A LIST

Sometimes it helps to make a list of things to write about. And sometimes it helps to make a list of the silliest, dumbest ideas you can think of. If you keep writing down silly ideas, some of them will turn out to be more interesting than you first thought.

Sometimes writing is easy. Sometimes writing is work. Either way, writing makes you more creative. And when you write, you create something that will always be yours.

Writer's Guide

Have you ever wondered where writers find ideas to write about? Or how they choose one idea if they have a dozen good ones? Have you ever struggled over the best way to put your ideas in order so that your writing will be clear for your readers? This Writer's Guide can answer these and other questions you have about writing.

Much of your writing is done in school. Many of the tips in this Guide are things you can do with your classmates. You can use the other tips by yourself.

Make Plans

People plan for everything. They plan trips; they plan what to do every day; they plan cities and towns; they plan for the future. Planning something makes doing it a lot easier.

It's the same with writing. Planning is just about the most important part of writing. Putting your ideas in order before you start writing will make the writing itself easier to do. Here are some tips to help you with your planning.

If you can't think of something to write about, use your journal. The ideas you wrote down there are like coins saved in a bank. Now you can use them. Read your notes. List the ones that could be writing topics.

If you still can't think of a topic, work with your classmates. Sit with a group and brainstorm ideas. Then talk about these ideas. This will help you and your friends decide on topics for writing. The more ideas you brainstorm, the more topics you'll have to choose from.

Another important part of planning is making sure your topic isn't too big. A topic such as "Disasters" is pretty big. So you choose a certain type of disaster. Let's say you chose "Volcanoes." That's better, but it's still too big. So you narrow it to one volcano, such as Mt. St. Helens or Mt. Vesuvius. Now you've got a Goldilocks-sized topic: not too big, not too small—just right for you!

Now you have a topic. What will you say about it? It's time to make another list. Make notes of facts and ideas from your reading. Write down your own thoughts. Check your journal again. Plan what to say before you write. That way you will have plenty to write about.

Last, put your list in order. Plan what you will say first. Figure out which ideas come before or after others. This plan is like a map. It tells you where you are going. Then you can start.

Write Away!

• •

Now you're ready to follow your plan and start writing. Here are a few tips that will help you get started and keep going.

GET STARTED
Pick a place to work and get that place ready. You'll probably need sharp pencils, paper, your lists, a dictionary, and this thesaurus. Make sure you have enough light. It's best to work in a quiet place. A radio, television, or tape player won't help you write. If you have trouble finding a quiet place, ask your family or your teacher for help. Remember, the library in your neighborhood or at school is a quiet place.

When you write, be sure to give yourself enough time. Spend at least twenty or thirty minutes on your writing. You may not finish the job on the first day, but you'll get a good start. When you go back to your writing, make sure you allow yourself the same amount of time.

Read over your lists. Remind yourself of the order in which you want to say things. Think of an interesting first sentence. Now start!

Write as fast as you can. Leave extra space between lines. Don't worry about saying things exactly right the first time. After your ideas are down on paper, you can fix what needs fixing.

KEEP GOING
Oh, no! You got started all right, but now you've stopped again. Try these tips.

Reread what you've written so far. Maybe you'll get an idea for how to keep going. Read your last couple of sentences aloud and just keep talking. Write down what you say.

Reread your notes. Search for an idea, fact, or word that will help you get started again.

Do some revising. Working on what you have already written may help you get going again.

Skip ahead. Go to a later part of what you are writing and work on that. You can come back and fill in the missing section after you're done.

Start over. Writers often do this. You may be able to use parts of your first draft later.

Whatever you do, *don't* just sit there staring at the page. Stand up and turn around three times. Look up the last word you wrote in your dictionary. Choose any word at all and use it in your next sentence—but keep going!

Fix It Up

Writing is never perfect the first time. Even good writers have to revise. One famous writer said that she couldn't write five words without changing seven. You should expect to fix your writing too. This is your chance to make it even better.

Keep these tips in mind when you revise your writing.

Wait a while. Don't start revising as soon as you finish writing. You'll have a fresh outlook on your work when you go back to it.

When you're ready to revise, think about these questions:

- Do you start with a really strong sentence that grabs your reader?

- Have you used all the ideas from the list you made when you were planning?

- Does the order of your ideas make sense? Now you can see if your plan worked. If it didn't, plan again!

- Have you used words your reader knows?

- Have you used synonyms so you're not repeating the same words over and over?

Ask your teacher or a classmate what's not clear in your writing. They can suggest ways to improve what you've written.

Your paper can get pretty messy when you revise your writing. Make your changes in a different color pen or pencil, as shown below.

Firefighters ~~fought~~ battled the fire and saved three lives. ~~rescued some people~~.

This way you'll know what's original and what's new.

Clean It Up

When you finish revising, make a new copy. Last of all, proofread it. Check to make sure there aren't any mistakes. It can be hard to find mistakes in your own writing. If you can, have someone else read what you've written. Exchange writing with a classmate. Look for errors in spelling, capitalization, and punctuation.

If you need to make changes, use a colored pencil. This will make the changes easier to see.

When you finish proofreading, you're done!

Indexes

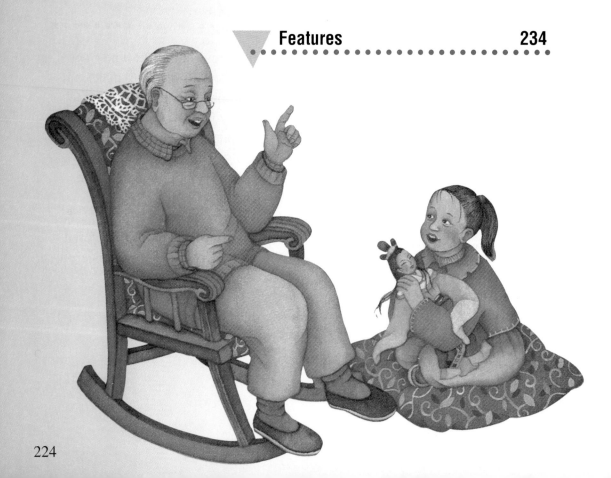

Synonym Index

Entry words are shown in darker type.

a hat	â care	ė term	o hot	ô order	u cup	ch child	th thin		a in about
ā age	e let	i it	ō open	oi oil	ù put	ng long	ŧH then	ə	e in taken / i in pencil
ä far	ē equal	ī ice	ȯ saw	ou out	ü rule	sh she	zh measure		o in lemon / u in circus

C

D

a hat	â care	ė term	o hot	ô order	u cup	ch child	th thin	a in about
ā age	e let	i it	ō open	oi oil	ú put	ng long	ᴛʜ then	e in taken
ä far	ē equal	ī ice	ȯ saw	ou out	ü rule	sh she	zh measure	ə i in pencil
								o in lemon
								u in circus

L

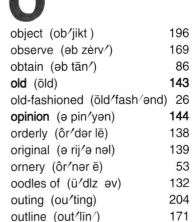

M

N

O

a	hat	â	care	ė	term	o	hot	ô	order	u	cup	ch	child	th	thin		a in about
ā	age	e	let	i	it	ō	open	oi	oil	u̇	put	ng	long	ᴛʜ	then	ə	e in taken i in pencil
ä	far	ē	equal	ī	ice	ȯ	saw	ou	out	ü	rule	sh	she	zh	measure		o in lemon u in circus

P

pace (pās) 210
pack (pak) 44
packed (pakt) 83
pain (pān) **145**
pal (pal) 82
pardon (pärd′n) 118
part (pärt) **146**
pastime (pas′tīm′) 150
penniless (pen′ē lis) 151
perceive (pər sēv′) 169
perfect (pėr′fikt) **147**
perform (pər fôrm′) 65
perilous (per′ə ləs) 60
petrified (pet′rə fīd′) 23
pick (pik) 48
piece (pēs) **148**
pitch (pich) 199
place (plās) 155
plain (plān) 69
plan (plan) **149**
play (plā) **150**
playmate (plā′māt′) 82
pleasant (plez′nt) 140
pledge (plej) 152
plod (plod) 210
plot (plot) 149
poky (pō′kē) 177
polished (pol′isht) 179
poor (pur) 34, **151**
portion (pôr′shən) 146
positive (poz′ə tiv) 187
poverty-stricken
　(pov′ər tē strik′ən) 151
powerful (pou′ər fəl) 184
prehistoric (prē′hi stôr′ik) 26
pretty (prit′ē) 36
prevent (pri vent′) 182
principal (prin′sə pəl) 130
problem (prob′ləm) 136
profile (prō′fīl) 171
program (prō′gram) 149
promise (prom′is) **152**
pronto (pron′tō) 186

propel (prə pel′) 154
protected (prə tek′tid) 165
pull (pul) **153**
pursue (pər sü′) 88
push (push) **154**
put (put) **155**
puzzle (puz′əl) 136

Q

quantity (kwon′tə tē) 25
quarrel (kwôr′əl) 29
question (kwes′chən) 31
quick (kwik) **156**
quiz (kwiz) 31

R

racket (rak′it) 142
radiant (rā′dē ənt) 42
raging (rāj′ing) 215
raid (rād) 32
ramble (ram′bəl) 89
rapid (rap′id) 156
reach (rēch) 50
realize (rē′ə līz) 114
reason (rē′zn) 198
recall (ri kol′) 158
receive (ri sēv′) 86
reckless (rek′lis) 43
reclaim (ri klām′) 166
recognize (rek′əg nīz) 114
recollect (rek′ə lekt′) 158
record (ri kôrd′) 190
release (ri lēs′) 119
remember (ri mem′bər) **158**
remove (ri müv′) 135
reply (ri plī′) 28
rescue (res′kyü) 166
reside (ri zīd′) 122
response (ri spons′) 28

retort (ri tôrt′) 28
reveal (ri vēl′) 119
revolve (ri volv′) 206
rich (rich) **159**
riddle (rid′l) 136
ridiculous (ri dik′yə ləs) 84
rim (rim) 72
rise (rīz) **160**
risky (ris′kē) 60
roam (rōm) 89
roar (rôr) 116
robust (rō bust′) 184
rotate (rō′tāt) 206
rotten (rot′n) 193
rough (ruf) 97, **161**
rove (rōv) 89
rowdy (rou′dē) 137
rugged (rug′id) 161
ruin (rü′ən) 62
rumpus (rum′pəs) 142
run (run) **162**
rush (rush) 106

S

sad (sad) **164**
safe (sāf) **165**
savage (sav′ij) 215
save (sāv) 113, **166**
saw (so) 57
say (sā) **167**
scale (skāl) 30
scare (skâr) **168**
scared (skârd) 23
scary (skâr′ē) 194
scheme (skēm) 149
scorching (skôr′ching) 103
scrap (skrap) 148
scream (skrēm) 172
secret (sē′krit) 136
section (sek′shən) 146
secure (si kyur′) 165
see (sē) **169**
segment (seg′mənt) 146

230

a	hat	â	care	ė	term	o	hot	ô	order	u	cup	ch	child	th	thin	ə	a in about
ā	age	e	let	i	it	ō	open	oi	oil	ů	put	ng	long	ᴛʜ	then		e in taken
ä	far	ē	equal	ī	ice	ò	saw	ou	out	ü	rule	sh	she	zh	measure		i in pencil
																	o in lemon
																	u in circus

a hat	â care	ė term	o hot	ô order	u cup	ch child	th thin	ə a in about
ā age	e let	i it	ō open	oi oil	ù put	ng long	ŦH then	e in taken
ä far	ē equal	ī ice	ȯ saw	ou out	ü rule	sh she	zh measure	i in pencil
								o in lemon
								u in circus

Idiom and Phrasal Verb Index

Features Index

Language Arts

▼ • • • • • • • • • • • • •

These features support the development of language arts and writing skills.

• • • • • • • • • • • • • •

P.S.

P.S. stands for "postscript," which is what we call something added at the end of a letter or any writing. You will find a P.S. at the end of each of the following studies:

adult	22
bad	34
break	41
carry	44
cold	49
come	50
cut	57
do	65
easy	69
fall	76
get	87
go	89
hold	102
hot	103
perfect	147
put	155
quick	156
shut	175
slow	177
take	191
talk	192
throw	199
turn	206

Enrichment

These features enrich and extend vocabulary development.

WORD POOLS

bright: flicker, gleam, glitter, shimmer, sparkle, twinkle 42

carry: airplane, barge, bicycle, boat, bus, car, cart, dogsled, freight train, handcart, motorcycle, pickup truck, shopping cart, train, truck, wagon, wheelbarrow 45

cute: calf, chick, cub, duckling, fawn, foal, gosling, kid, kitten, lamb, piglet, puppy 58

eat: bite, chew, chomp, feast, gnaw, gulp, munch, swallow, taste, wolf down 70

eat: bagel, baguette, bialy, biscuit, bun, challah, chapati, cornbread, cracker, croissant, crumpet, dumpling, English muffin, matzo, muffin, papadam, pita, popover, roll, scone, tortilla 71

go: crawl, creep, dance, glide, slide, slither, waddle, wade, wiggle, wriggle 89

group: brood, covey, flock, gaggle, herd, litter, pack, pod, pride, school, swarm 95

live: apartment building, cabin, cottage, farmhouse, hacienda, hogan, house, housing project, hut, igloo, kraal, mobile home, palace, pueblo, ranch house, shack, tepee, townhouse, villa, yurt 123

look: gape, gawk, glare, glower, goggle, ogle, peek, peer, survey, squint 125

many: billions, heaps, jillions, loads, millions, scads, tons, trillions, umpteen, zillions 132

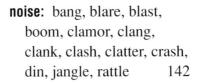

noise: bang, blare, blast, boom, clamor, clang, clank, clash, clatter, crash, din, jangle, rattle 142

noise: hum, mumble, murmur, patter, purr, rustle, sigh, swish, whisper 142

run: bolt, dart, dash, gallop, jog, lope, race, scamper, scoot, scurry, sprint, trot 163

say: affirm, announce, assert, assure, blurt, comment, cry, insist, mention, mumble, murmur, mutter, proclaim, remark, report, relate, scream, whisper 167

shape: circle, cone, cube, diamond, hexagon, octagon, oval, pentagon, pyramid, rectangle, sphere, square, triangle 171

shout: bellow, cheer, groan, holler, howl, roar, screech, squawk, squeal, thunder, wail, whoop, yelp 172

story: autobiography, ballad, biography, epic, fable, fairy tale, folklore, legend, mystery, myth, novel, parable, romance, science fiction, western 183

walk: amble, clump, hike, hobble, limp, lumber, lurch, pad, prance, saunter, shamble, stagger, stalk, stamp, stroll, strut, stumble, swagger, tiptoe, totter, tramp, tread, trip, trudge 211

wet: bay, bayou, bog, brook, canal, channel, cove, creek, gulf, lagoon, lake, marsh, ocean, pond, pool, puddle, river, sea, spring, stream, strait, sound, swamp, waterfall, whirlpool 213

Literature

This feature uses authentic literature to showcase word choice.

Literature

▽

This feature uses authentic literature to showcase word choice.

WRITER'S CHOICE

Matura, Mustapha *Moon Jump* 104

Uchida, Yoshiko *Sumi & the Goat & the Tokyo Express* 188

Asimov, Isaac *What Makes the Sun Shine?* 153

Mohr, Nicholasa *Going Home* 165

Yep, Laurence *The Star Fisher* 28

Keller, Beverly *Only Fiona* 53

Myers, Walter Dean *Me, Mop, and the Moondance Kid* 211

Yount, Lisa *Black Scientists* 79

Landau, Elaine *Cowboys* 24

Sobol, Donald J. *Encyclopedia Brown's Book of Wacky Cars* 40

Lawlor, Laurie *Addie's Dakota Winter* 64

Taylor, Mildred D. *The Friendship* 124

Art Credits

Unless otherwise credited, all photographs are the property of Scott, Foresman and Company.

p. 3 LeeLee Brazeal
p. 21 Mary Jones
p. 23 Don Wilson
p. 25 LeeLee Brazeal
p. 26-27 Robert J. Lee
p. 29 Chi Chung
p. 30 Leslie Cober
p. 31 Chi Chung
p. 32 LeeLee Brazeal
p. 33 LeeLee Brazeal
p. 34 Mary Jones
p. 35 Ellen Joy Sasaki
p. 36 Leslie Cober
p. 37 LeeLee Brazeal
p. 38-39 Rob Barber
p. 40 Leslie Cober
p. 41 Leslie Cober
p. 42 Kathi Ember
p. 43 Chi Chung
p. 44 LeeLee Brazeal
p. 45 (TL) M & E Bernheim/Woodfin Camp and Associates
(TCL) Kim Heacox/Peter Arnold, Inc.
(TR) Superstock
(CL) Superstock
(CR) Superstock
(BL) Superstock
(BR) Superstock
p. 46 LeeLee Brazeal
p. 47 LeeLee Brazeal
p. 48-49 Rob Barber
p. 50 Ellen Joy Sasaki
p. 51 Mary Jones
p. 52 Kathi Ember
p. 54-55 Linda Kelen
p. 56 Leslie Cober
p. 58 (L) Larry Lefever/ Grant Heilman Photography
(TC) Y. Arthus-Bertrand/Peter Arnold Inc.
(TR) George H. Harrison/Grant Heilman Photography
(BL) Hans Reinhard/Bruce Coleman Inc.
(BR) Frank Oberle/ Bruce Coleman Inc.
p. 60 Ann-Marie Weber/ The Stock Market
p. 61 Patricia Barbee
p. 62 Rob Barber
p. 63 Superstock
p. 64 Roni Shepherd
p. 65 Don Wilson
p. 66 LeeLee Brazeal
p. 67 LeeLee Brazeal
p. 69 Mary Jones
p. 70 LeeLee Brazeal
p. 72 Patricia Barbee

p. 73 Leslie Cober
p. 74 Mary Jones
p. 75 Rick Stewart/ Allsport USA
p. 76-77 Mary Jones
p. 76 Death of General Mercer at the Battle of Princeton by John Trumbull/Yale University Art Gallery
p. 79 Mary Jones
p. 80-81 Robert J. Lee
p. 82 Comstock
p. 83 Leslie Cober
p. 84-85 Rob Barber
p. 87 Rob Barber
p. 88 Ellen Joy Sasaki
p. 89 Tony Stone Images
p. 90 Leslie Cober
p. 91 Leslie Cober
p. 92 Rob Barber
p. 93 Still Life by Fantin-Latour/Courtesy National Gallery of Art
p. 94 (TL) Grant Heilman/ Grant Heilman Photography
(TR) Simon Trevor/ Bruce Coleman Inc.
(BL) Jane Burton/ Bruce Coleman Inc.
(BR) Gerard Lacz/ Peter Arnold, Inc.
p. 95 (T) Gerard Lacz/ Peter Arnold Inc.
(CL) Larry Lipski/ Bruce Coleman Inc.
(C) Dr. Eckart Pott/ Bruce Coleman Inc.
(CR) Gerard Lacz/ Peter Arnold Inc.
(BL) Grant Heilman/ Grant Heilman Photography
(BR) John H. Hoffman/Bruce Coleman Inc.
p. 96 Chi Chung
p. 97 Gary Moore/ Mountain Stock
p. 98 Mary Jones
p. 99 Kathi Ember
p. 100 Ellen Joy Sasaki
p. 101 Ellen Joy Sasaki
p. 103 Rob Barber
p. 105 John Eggert
p. 106 Mary Jones
p. 107 Leslie Cober
p. 108 John Eggert
p. 109 John Eggert
p. 110 Leslie Cober
p. 111 Leslie Cober
p. 112 Rob Barber
p. 113 Patricia Barbee
p. 114 Courtesy The National Theatre for the Deaf
p. 115 Mary Jones
p. 117 Rob Barber
p. 118 Mary Jones
p. 119 John Eggert
p. 120 LeeLee Brazeal
p. 121 LeeLee Brazeal
p. 122 (BR) William Strode/ Woodfin Camp & Associates
p. 123 (C) Ken Dequaine/ Third Coast Stock Source
(B) Chris Cross/ Uniphoto
p. 125 Rob Barber
p. 126 Rob Barber
p. 127 Superstock
p. 128 Linda Kelen
p. 129 Linda Kelen
p. 131 Rob Barber
p. 132 LeeLee Brazeal
p. 133 LeeLee Brazeal
p. 134 Leslie Cober
p. 135 Leslie Cober
p. 136-137 Don Wilson
p. 138 Mary Jones
p. 139 Rob Barber
p. 140 Kathi Ember
p. 141 Kathi Ember
p. 142 Ellen Joy Sasaki
p. 143 Matthew Neal McVay/Tony Stone Images
p. 144 Chi Chung
p. 145 Mary Jones
p. 146 Rob Barber
p. 147 Reuters/Bettmann
p. 148 Leslie Cober
p. 149 Patricia Barbee
p. 150 Don Wilson
p. 152 Linda Kelen
p. 154 LeeLee Brazeal
p. 155 LeeLee Brazeal
p. 157 Patricia Barbee
p. 158 Ellen Joy Sasaki
p. 159 Rob Barber
p. 160 S.J. Kraseman/ Peter Arnold Inc.
p. 161 Kurt Scholz/ Superstock
p. 162 Roni Shepherd
p. 163 Ellen Joy Sasaki
p. 164 Mary Jones
p. 165 Mary Jones
p. 166 Rob Barber
p. 168 LeeLee Brazeal
p. 169 LeeLee Brazeal
p. 170 Leslie Cober
p. 171 Craig Aurness / Westlight/ Woodfin Camp and Associates
p. 172 Chi Chung
p. 173 Rob Barber
p. 174 Ellen Joy Sasaki
p. 175 Ellen Joy Sasaki
p. 176 Rob Barber
p. 177 Kathi Ember
p. 178 Patricia Barbee
p. 180 Jeff Foott
p. 181 Courtesy NASA
p. 182 Jenny Moulton/Tony Stone Images
p. 183 Chi Chung
p. 184 Ellen Joy Sasaki
p. 185 Ellen Joy Sasaki
p. 186 John Eggert
p. 187 Rob Barber
p. 188-189 Don Wilson

p. 190 Charles Tasnadi/AP/ Wide World Photos
p. 192 Ellen Joy Sasaki
p. 193 Rob Barber
p. 194 LeeLee Brazeal
p. 195 Ellen Joy Sasaki
p. 196-197 Don Wilson
p. 198-199 Rob Barber
p. 201 (T) Runk/ Schoenberger/ Grant Heilman Photography
(C) L.S. Stepanowicz/Bruce Coleman Inc.
(B) L.S. Stepanowicz/Bruce Coleman Inc.
p. 202 LeeLee Brazeal
p. 203 LeeLee Brazeal
p. 204 David Austen/Tony Stone Images
p. 205 (TL) Courtesy NASA
(TR) Catherine Koehler
(B) Murray & Associates/ Tony Stone Images
p. 206 Gamma-Liaison
p. 207 Mary Jones
p. 208 LeeLee Brazeal
p. 209 LeeLee Brazeal
p. 210-211 Kathi Ember
p. 212 Leslie Cober
p. 213 Roni Shepherd
p. 214 Rob Barber
p. 215 Terry Sirrell
p. 216 Superstock
p. 217 Patricia Barbee
p. 220 Linda Kelen
p. 224 Chi Chung
p. 226 Larry Lefever/Grant Heilman Photography
p. 227 Robert J. Lee
p. 229 Rob Barber
LeeLee Brazeal
p. 232 Ellen Joy Sasaki
p. 233 Roni Shepherd
p. 234 Leslie Cober
p. 235 LeeLee Brazeal
p. 236 Rob Barber
p. 237 Ellen Joy Sasaki

Alphabet Letters A-W:
Susan Swan

Cover Art
Front: Patricia Barbee, Rob Barber, LeeLee Brazeal, Chi Chung, Leslie Cober, Mary Jones, Ellen Joy Sasaki

Back: Rob Barber, LeeLee Brazeal, Mary Jones, Ellen Joy Sasaki, Roni Sheperd

Acknowledgments

Asimov, Isaac, WHAT MAKES THE SUN SHINE?
Boston: Little, Brown, and Company, 1971, p. 6. 153

Keller, Beverly, ONLY FIONA. New York: Harper and
Row Publishers, 1988, p. 9. 53

Landau, Elaine, COWBOYS. New York: Franklin Watts,
1990, p. 22. 24

Lawlor, Laurie, ADDIE'S DAKOTA WINTER. Niles,
Illinois: Albert Whitman and Company, 1989, p. 14.
64

Matura, Mustapha, MOON JUMP. New York: Alfred A.
Knopf, 1988, p.12. 104

Mohr, Nicholasa, GOING HOME. New York: Dial Books
for Young Readers, 1986, p. 54. 165

Myers, Walter Dean, ME, MOP, AND THE MOON-
DANCE KID. New York: Delacorte Press, 1988,
p. 61–62. 211

Sobol, Donald J., ENCYCLOPEDIA BROWN'S BOOK
OF WACKY CARS. New York: William Morrow
and Company, Inc., 1987, p. 32. 40

Taylor, Mildred D., THE FRIENDSHIP. New York: Dial
Books for Young Readers, 1987, p. 12. 124

Uchida, Yoshiko, SUMI & THE GOAT & THE TOKYO
EXPRESS. New York: Charles Scribner's Sons,
1969, p. 16. 188

Yep, Laurence, THE STAR FISHER. New York:
Morrow Junior Books, 1991, p. 160. 28

Yount, Lisa, BLACK SCIENTISTS. New York: Facts on
File, 1991, p. 86. 79

Credits

From "A New Song to Sing About Jonathan Bing" by
Beatrice Curtis Brown from JONATHAN BING. Text
copyright © 1968 by Beatrice Curtis Brown.
Copyright 1936 by Oxford University Press.
Copyright © 1964 by Beatrice Curtis Brown.
Reprinted by permission of Curtis Brown Ltd.

"Ho-Hum" and "And They Met in the Middle" from THE
HOPEFUL TROUT AND OTHER LIMERICKS by
John Ciardi. Text copyright © 1989 by Myra J. Ciardi.
Reprinted by permission of Houghton Mifflin
Company. All rights reserved.

Excerpt from ALL UPON A SIDEWALK by Jean
Craighead George. Copyright © 1974 by Jean
Craighead George. Reprinted by permission of Curtis
Brown, Ltd.

Lucia & James Hymes, Jr., OODLES OF NOODLES, ©
1964 by Addison-Wesley Publishing Company.
Reprinted with permission of the publisher.

"Sardines" from A BOOK OF MILLIGANIMALS by
Spike Milligan. Reprinted by permission of Spike
Milligan Productions Ltd.